CREATIVE
HOMEOWNER®

Eat-In Kitchens

Inspiration for Updating an American Classic

Catherine Warren Leone

CREATIVE HOMEOWNER®, Upper Saddle River, New Jersey

EAT-IN KITCHENS

SENIOR EDITOR	Kathie Robitz
EDITOR	Lisa Kahn
SENIOR GRAPHIC DESIGN COORDINATOR	Glee Barre
PHOTO COORDINATOR	Robyn Poplasky
DIGITAL IMAGING SPECIALIST	Frank Dyer
INDEXER	Schroeder Indexing Services
COVER DESIGN	Glee Barre
ILLUSTRATIONS	Glee Barre
FRONT COVER PHOTOGRAPHY	Mark Samu; (top right) design: Jean Stoffer Design; (bottom right) design Durst Construction; (left) design: Big Designs
BACK COVER PHOTOGRAPHY	Mark Samu; (bottom left) Big Designs; (bottom center and bottom right) design: Jean Stoffer Design

CREATIVE HOMEOWNER

VICE PRESIDENT AND PUBLISHER	Timothy O. Bakke
PRODUCTION DIRECTOR	Kimberly H. Vivas
ART DIRECTOR	David Geer
MANAGING EDITOR	Fran J. Donegan

Current Printing (last digit)
10 9 8 7 6 5 4 3 2 1

Eat-In Kitchens, First Edition
Library of Congress Control Number: 2007942991
ISBN-10: 1-58011-412-1
ISBN-13: 978-1-58011-412-7

Manufactured in the United States of America

CREATIVE HOMEOWNER®
A Division of Federal Marketing Corp.
24 Park Way
Upper Saddle River, NJ 07458
www.creativehomeowner.com

Planet Friendly Publishing
✓ Made in the United States
✓ Printed on Recycled Paper
Learn more at www.greenedition.org

GREEN EDITION

At Creative Homeowner we're committed to producing books in an earth-friendly manner and to helping our customers make greener choices.

Manufacturing books in the United States ensures compliance with strict environmental laws and eliminates the need for international freight shipping, a major contributor to global air pollution.

Printing on recycled paper also helps minimize our consumption of trees, water, and fossil fuels. *Eat-In Kitchens* was printed on paper made with 10% post-consumer waste. According to Environmental Defense's Paper Calculator, by using this innovative paper instead of conventional papers, we achieved the following environmental benefits:

Trees Saved: 30

Water Saved: 10,762 gallons

Solid Waste Eliminated: 1,781 pounds

Air Emissions Eliminated: 3,283 pounds

For more information on our environmental practices, please visit us online at www.creativehomeowner.com/green

dedication

To Frank and Frankie and Cissy

acknowledgments

Much thanks to my delightful book genies, Editor Lisa Kahn and Senior Designer Glee Barre, who seem to have conjured up this gorgeous book by simply smiling and twitching their noses.

Contents

Introduction

Often bustling but always welcoming, the new eat-in kitchen is a microcosm of the way families live. Instead of using walls to divide people and activities, the modern eat-in kitchen is an open, versatile space—a domestic crossroads where family and friends gather to cook, eat, share, and live the good life. A room that performs so many important functions requires meticulous planning and careful budgeting. It can be a challenge, but one that will provide pleasure for many years to come. In these pages, you'll find help and inspiration for every step of the process, from design and layout to selecting the finishes, cabinetry, appliances, and accessories that will perfectly suit your very own eat-in kitchen.

chapter 1

eat-in central

The center of life at home, the eat-in kitchen makes room for cook, friends, and family to gather and interact.

Referring to the modern do-it-all kitchen as "Eat-In Central" is no overstatement. It's here that **daily meals** are **prepared** and served, toddlers **play**, teens do their **homework,** and parents **pay bills.** Eat-In Central is the casual, welcoming **heart** of today's **home.** It's a **place** where cooking, serving, cleanup, and most important, your **loved ones** are always close at hand.

BELOW Complemented by stylish stools, the long stretch of island enables guests and family to chat with the cook. The adjacent dining area brings in the outdoors.

OPPOSITE The eat-in kitchen (also pictured below) is the focus of this comfortable great room, which is designed for casual entertaining. The prep station faces the living area, ensuring that the cook is part of the action.

History Repeats Itself

The concept of the eat-in kitchen has expanded and contracted over the centuries, coming full circle from colonial times, when family life revolved around the fire in the corner of the cabin's largest—if not only—room.

Today, both the living quarters and the lifestyle of the average family are far more sophisticated than those of our forebears. Yet the appeal of a single, multipurpose space to cook, eat, and conduct most family and social interactions has never been greater. Part of this resurgence has to do with a penchant for the convenience of having everything—and everyone—in one place. Rather than herding guests off to a formal dining room while the cook chops vegetables behind closed doors, dinner can now be a participatory sport where, from their seats at a nearby table or center island, everyone can play a part in the action.

Naturally, you'll need to carefully consider how your eat-in kitchen will affect the view, layout, and flow to the rest of your home.

Designed to Serve

The best dream kitchens are based on hard realities, such as setting a budget and doing lots of careful planning. To stay on track, add a cushion for unforeseen expenses and then resist the urge to tack on more here and there as the project progresses. Start your planning process by dissecting all of the kitchens you've known firsthand from childhood to the present. Make a list of what you think worked and what didn't.

Next, ask questions of yourself and the experts. How much room do you want, and how much do you actually need? Which countertop and flooring materials require the most

let's DISH

ABOUT THE DESIGN PROS

- Architects plan, design, and oversee construction; they're necessary for an addition or renovation.

- Certified kitchen designers (CKDs) are trained in all aspects of kitchen design, from layout to plumbing.

- Interior designers create the visual look; not all have kitchen–design experience, so be sure to ask.

- General contractors work from plans drawn up by another pro; they oversee the day-to-day work on the project permits, cabinetry, plumbing, and the works.

ABOVE The island cooking zone takes center stage; on the sidelines, a peninsula snack center serves family and friends.

OPPOSITE LEFT A bright and sunny view from the sink is an enduring element in upscale kitchen design.

OPPOSITE RIGHT The kitchen island makes a bold design statement while also increasing countertop and storage space.

DID YOU KNOW?

Acting like a kid–at least for the moment–can pay off when planning your new kitchen. Pretend to cook, cleanup, and serve a meal in your new floor plan. Open the cabinets; use the appliances; and work at the sink. Make sure you aren't taking too many steps.

maintenance? The least? Do you yearn for natural light? Better task lighting? What are your family's needs now and what will they be in the future? Are there multiple cooks?

Do you require special zones for grilling and baking? For entertaining? For computing the family finances? Does the existing configuration make sense? Can the space be opened up by removing one or more walls, or by incorporating adjacent space? Is there room on your property—and in your budget—for building an addition? Study your family's individual needs. For example, is there an exceptionally short (or tall) family member who is uncomfortable working at a standard-height counter? Do you want a window with a view of the yard? Will you be able to easily unload groceries from the car and dispose of trash? Are the front and back doors within reach?

Explore model kitchens. Talk to designers and sales people. Look at the latest appliances, and record their dimensions. When you're ready, take a box of chalk into the garage or basement and sketch the full-scale design on the floor. There are some surprises nobody wants—such as cabinets and counters that, once installed, look nothing like what you expected. The best prevention is to see as much as you can before work begins.

let's DISH

A BUDGET GUIDELINE
Here is an estimate of how much of your money goes where during a kitchen construction project.

- 40% cabinets

- 15% appliances

- 15% countertops

- 16% labor

- 6% design

- 5% flooring

- 3% fixtures

Carefully search for potential **safety hazards** in your kitchen design. An **oven door** shouldn't open into a **high-traffic area**. Plan for adequate **landing space** on either side of **cooktops** for quick placement of **hot pots and pans**.

Ergonomic kitchens work for their users: appliances are close to one another to reduce the cook's fatigue, and adequate pathways allow room for traffic and seating.

If small children are often in the kitchen, special lockout features on ovens and other appliances are good safety measures. When placing kitchen equipment, let ergonomics be your guide so that sinks, stoves, and counters won't be too high or too low.

let's DISH

Everything in Its Place

In Eat-In Central, special areas dedicated to a family's daily needs guarantee that there's a place for everyone and everything. These zones may include a pantry, an entertainment area, a kids' activity spot, an office space, and even a charging station for cell phones and other electronics. But the most important zones by far are the hard-working areas used for food prep, cooking, and cleanup. For generations, these areas were arranged in the time-tested work triangle, considered the gold standard of efficiency for positioning the sink, stove, and refrigerator. However, the classic triangle may not be the most streamlined approach for today's eat-in kitchen, especially if

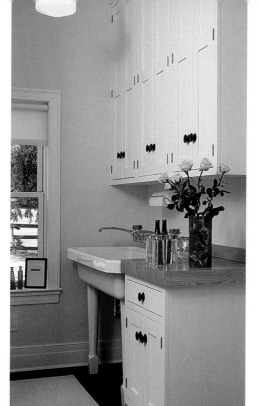

OPPOSITE The beauty of simplicity and function combine in a streamlined kitchen where areas for prep work, cooking, and cleanup, as well as storage, flow gracefully from one to the other.

LEFT In addition to storage space, this area adjacent to the kitchen provides a smaller secondary sink and extra counter space.

BELOW For easy entertaining, outfit a wall near the island counter with a small bar, cabinet, and wine rack.

> **DID YOU KNOW?**
> The walk-in pantry is the most often requested addition to a kitchen floor plan.

BELOW This curved granite island offers dining space for four, in addition to generous prep space for the cook on the opposite side.

OPPOSITE A gleaming professional range is a good fit in any style kitchen.

your plans include cooking stations for more than one cook. If so, you might want to consider some alternative layouts.

Primary Kitchen Zones

It's likely that there was just one of everything in your grandmother's kitchen, an arrangement that worked well because she was probably the sole cook. Grandma used the sink area for both food preparation and cleanup, and kept bowls, pots, and other utensils within easy reach of the stove and refrigerator.

Things are quite different in today's Eat-In Central. We still want plenty of workspace close to the sink. But the increasing number of gadgets, appliances, and cooks in the kitchen now call for multiple use zones.

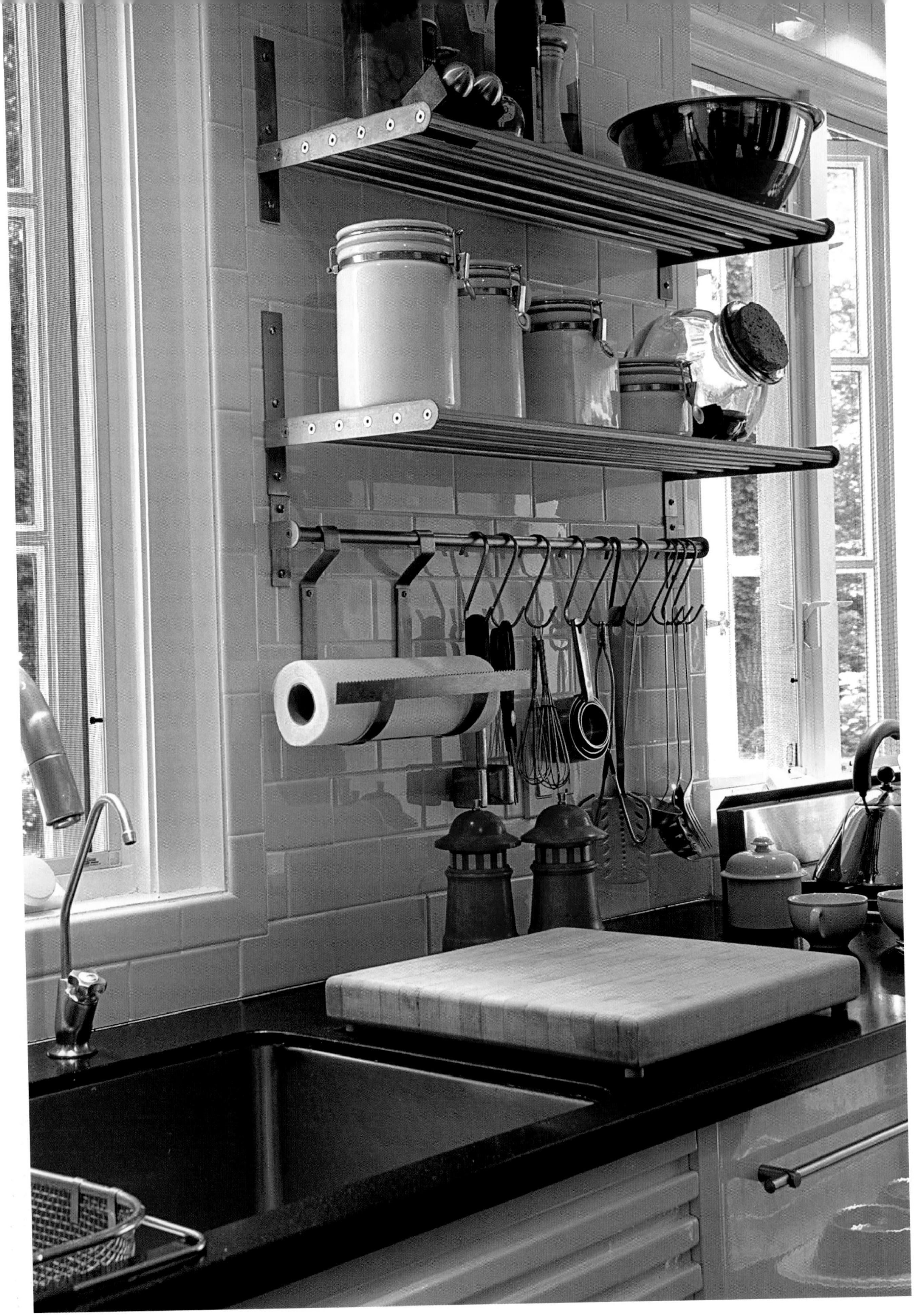

The Prep Zone

The kitchen sink and its surrounding counter space and storage areas are the prep zone's crucial components. In larger spaces, there can be multiple prep centers; each with its own sink, work space, and storage, plus a smaller, dedicated refrigerator for each center. The island is often an integral part of the prep zone and can offer multiple counter heights to accommodate each cook. For efficiency's sake, the prep zone should be close to staples and condiments, dishes, pots and pans, and cooking utensils. In addition to housing the refrigerator, the prep zone should also include a microwave and garbage disposal, recycling bins, small appliances, and drinking-water dispensers.

A walk-in pantry is the most frequently requested addition to a kitchen floor plan. This may be true because today's open-kitchen designs often sacrifice upper cabinets along with the precious storage space they offer. The pantry may be located in the kitchen or an adjacent area.

OPPOSITE A compact prep zone makes good use of its subway-tiled wall, adding open shelving to hold frequently used items and installing a bar to hang whisks, measuring cups, and other utensils.

BELOW The undermounted sink is an excellent choice for the prep zone. Because there are no messy rims to trap food residue and bacteria, cleanup is easier and more sanitary.

let's DISH

PREP PROFUSION
Specialty prep spots are springing up in today's kitchens, answering the need for separate spaces when two or more are at work. Among these small designated areas, which are meant to control prep traffic, is the breakfast prep station. Outfitted with small appliances, this out-of-the-mainstream spot works for making coffee and smoothies. While a parent makes breakfast at the main prep spot, one of the children can be at work at the sandwich (or, in the evening, appetizer) prep spot, packing school lunches.

{ **DID YOU KNOW?**
Many new hoods
provide features
such as utensil
racks, spice
storage, and
mood lighting. }

The Cooking Zone

Beautiful ventilation hoods over professional-style ranges have earned the cooking zone an aesthetic place of honor in the kitchen. Besides the range, other cooking-zone appliances may include warming drawers or heat lamps, a microwave, ovens, and an additional sink or pot filler. Pots and pans, cooking utensils, spices, and condiments can be tucked away within easy reach in good-looking pullout drawers and shelves.

LEFT Not only does the design simplicity of the stainless-steel hood complement the room's neutral color scheme, it functions as wall art in this streamlined kitchen.

TOP RIGHT This stainless-steel hood serves as a stylish counterpoint to the warm brick backsplash and the professional range in this contemporary kitchen.

BOTTOM RIGHT The only way to completely remove cooking odors and greasy air is with a hooded exhaust system that vents to the outdoors. This geometric-shaped hood in stainless steel perfectly integrates itself into the kitchen's clean-lined design.

let's DISH

INVESTIGATE YOUR OPTIONS

- Learn the language of kitchen design. Familiarize yourself with the pros and cons of design layouts and kitchen essentials.
- Investigate the latest appliances, materials, and fixtures at kitchen shows and stores; learn about their technology and available styles and color.
- Visit manufacturer Web sites and save images of layouts that work for your space.
- Talk to friends and family who have renovated or added a new kitchen. What things do they love about it? What would they have done differently?
- Make a list of the absolute necessities you can't live without in your new kitchen. What must you have? What would simply be great to have?
- Prioritize these needs and wishes; then console yourself with the knowledge that it probably wouldn't all fit, anyway.

LEFT The wall-installed grill is close to the hood, making grease an easy target for removal.

RIGHT This stainless-steel hood looks like a piece of modern sculpture in counterpoint to warm wood and stone materials used in this casual kitchen.

BELOW Twin gooseneck faucets and a matching hot-water dispenser line up side by side on this limestone countertop.

OPPOSITE BELOW A professional-style faucet with a pull-down sprayer perches above a double sink.

OPPOSITE TOP RIGHT A small sink in the marble island creates a secondary work zone.

The Cleanup Zone

The sink is the center of attention in the cleanup zone, and today's eat-in kitchens certainly don't skimp on sinks and other water sources. There may be a prep sink and a bar sink, as well as a pot-filler faucet near the stove. Flanking the sink in the cleanup zone are conveniences such as pullout waste containers, recycling centers, and dishwashers.

The latest sink styles are bigger than ever and often use apron fronts that emphasize their increased size. While stainless-steel finishes continue to

proliferate, single-bowl styles are also surfacing in stone, copper, and enamel on cast iron. New hands-free faucets use electronic sensors to prevent the spread of germs and automatically turn off water when hands are removed. If there's only one sink in the kitchen, it's usually placed between the cooktop and the refrigerator. A countertop with a minimum width of 24 inches should flank the sink on one side, with a minimum width of 18 inches on the other side. To make short work of putting away dishes, storage space should be within 72 inches of the sink's center.

let's DISH

FAUCET FACTS

- Once exclusive, brushed-nickel and oil-rubbed bronze finishes are now available on more affordable faucets. Look for PVD (physical vapor deposition) finishes on the outside and ceramic discs on the inside.
- Chrome is the least-expensive faucet material.
- Easy-care stainless-steel faucets remain the most popular with homeowners.
- A brass finish requires frequent cleaning.
- Wall-mounted faucets keep the countertop clear, which makes cleanup easier.
- Work hands-free with motion activated or pedal-operated faucets.
- The best faucets offer lifetime protection against leaks and drips.
- While the majority of kitchen faucets fit all kitchen sinks, be sure to check sizes.
- High gooseneck faucets make filling large pots a cinch.

let's DISH

STONE COMPOSITES

Like countertops and floors, sinks can be made of good-looking and durable composite materials. **Polyester/acrylic** is the most affordable of the big three composite materials, but it scratches and stains easily. Still, its glossy surface and bright colors are major pluses. **Quartz composite,** a mixture of crushed quartz and resin fillers, resists most stains and scratches. Moderately priced, it comes in earth tones and brights. **Granite composite,** a mixture of crushed granite and resin fillers, is the most costly and durable of the composites. It's available in a range of colors and neutrals.

The Kitchen Sink

One of the most-used items in the kitchen, a good-quality sink should last as long as 30 years. A large, one-basin sink works well if you wash everything in the dishwasher. But if you find that you hand wash a number of items, a two- or even three-basin sink might make the most sense. **Extra-deep kitchen sinks** are available for those who often cook with oversize pots. **Stainless-steel sinks** have been popular for nearly a century because they're durable, easy to clean, and resist corrosion. You can reduce the cost of purchasing a stainless-steel sink by selecting a thinner, 23-gauge model rather than the more expensive 18-gauge one. (The higher the number, the thinner the metal.) According to many experts, these less-expensive versions resist heat and dents just as well as the pricier models. Stainless steel is available in either a polished or matte finish. **Porcelain enamel on cast iron,** equally as long-lived, comes in a broad range of styles and colors. **Metals, such as nickel and copper,** are beautiful but more expensive. Nickel is the harder of the two metals; pure copper requires no maintenance. Relatively new **composite sinks** are lighter than cast iron and have a smooth or textured finish. The most durable composites contain a higher percentage of quartz. While they look and feel like enamel, they are easier to clean because they are less porous.

Installation Styles

Self-rimming or drop-in sinks are set into the countertop with their edges overlapping the counter. They are inexpensive and available in most materials. Their drawback is that debris collects easily under the rim.

Undermounted sinks attach below the countertop. There are no visible edges, which creates a smooth and easy-to-clean surface. The surrounding countertop should be water resistant to avoid buckling or warping. Exposed-apron sinks are undermounted but reveal the sink's front panel. They can be made from most sink materials.

Integral sinks, made of the same material as the counter, are seamless and can be cleaned easily. Integral sinks can be fabricated of any flexible material, including stainless steel, solid surfacing, composites, and concrete.

OPPOSITE LEFT This aged-copper bowl mounted above the counter gives this sink a unique and stylish point of view; it is perfectly partnered with a faucet that reflects the patina of age.

OPPOSITE RIGHT An exposed-apron sink adds a nostalgic yet sleek note to this contemporary kitchen.

ABOVE An undermounted sink in the marble-top island is a convenient backup to the main kitchen sink.

Auxiliary Zones

Eat-in Central is a multifunctional space with a variety of additional zones that go beyond the basics. These may address the home chef's special culinary interests, or they can be spots for doing homework, paying bills, or support for other activities that have nothing to do with cooking.

The Baking Zone

The baking zone features lowered counters and storage for mixers, cookie sheets, and cake pans for the dedicated creator of breads and cakes.

TOP LEFT A favorite mixing bowl can be neatly stored in this work island.

ABOVE Cool marble, the perfect surface for rolling out dough, tops a compact cabinet for storing baking equipment.

OPPOSITE TOP The home office makes a functional and attractive transition between the kitchen and living area, putting intervening wall space to efficient use with a desk, computer, and comfortable chair.

OPPOSITE BOTTOM Clever design can turn a little bit of space into a work area simply by adding bookshelves, a desk with drawers, and a stool.

The Homework Zone

It's an area that can work as a place for kids to study their spelling or for parents to telecommute to the office and sort out home finances. A computer in the kitchen just makes life a little easier. Simply add an ergonomic chair and a height-adjustable keyboard tray. Plot outlet locations for the desktop computer area when you plan the electricity for the kitchen.

{ **DID YOU KNOW?**
Among families with children ages 6 to 11,
56 percent ate a meal together
six to seven days a week, and 25 percent
shared a meal together 4 to 5 days a week. }

LEFT This workstation features electrical outlets underneath the desk for recharging cell phones as well as natural and task lighting for getting down to business.

BELOW LEFT A small cubby is a perfect drop-off spot for juicing up the family's techno-gadgetry.

BELOW Integrated with the kitchen cabinetry, this well-equipped space has enough room to stay and work awhile.

OPPOSITE Even small children can help with meal prep if a freezer drawer and cabinets are at the right level.

The Charging Zone

This area of the kitchen can also be called "Techno Central." It's the spot where all of the family's electronic appliances, including cell phones, mp3 players, laptops, digital cameras, e-books, and all the must-have gadgets yet to be invented can be recharged and restored. Not only does this space keep everything running smoothly, but—perhaps best of all—it also takes the guess work out of finding your stuff as you're rushing out the door.

The Kids' Zone

A designated child-friendly space keeps little ones in plain sight yet safely out of the way of kitchen traffic. An area with a lowered countertop or small table (both with rounded edges rather than sharp corners) and an easy-to-reach cabinet or cubby for storing crayons, coloring books, and favorite toys can make kids part of the action in Eat-In Central. If a high chair needs a place at the table, leave at least 4 square feet for it in the floor plan. As a safety precaution, hold off on adding stools at high counters until children are old enough to sit on them safely without taking a tumble.

DID YOU KNOW?
Kids love doing things for themselves. Why not add a refrigerator drawer at their level so they can find their favorite snacks and treats?

BELOW The tiered island—a prep zone camouflaged by a higher level—works smoothly for entertaining, especially when there's plenty of space for family and friends to either sit or move around the room.

Entertainment Zone

The entertainment zone replaces the outdated concept of the wet bar. Because guests invariably end up in the kitchen anyway, consider a separate island outside the main work triangle that can be set up for coffee, cocktails, or a casual buffet. The entertainment zone might also feature a small refrigerator or wine cooler, a built-in espresso maker, and a food-warming drawer. Include storage for barware, dishes, flatware, serving bowls, and trays.

RIGHT Though small, this kitchen features a wide granite island with enough space for prep work and for comfortably entertaining guests. The floor-to-ceiling blackboard and large steel-rimmed clock lend a cozy bistro atmosphere.

The eat-in kitchen is at its **relaxing best** when it makes a **smooth** transition from the **cooking area** to a **nearby space** that promises— and **delivers**— comfort. Create a **bridge** between the two spaces with an **island,** a piece of **furniture,** or a **desk.**

Relaxation Zone

Give family and friends a place to sit and enjoy the moment. A small space can host a window seat or cozy nook; a larger space can accommodate a seating arrangement of sofa and chairs. Keep guests occupied while you cook by providing snacks and a selection of music from your mp3 playlist.

BELOW Light pours through tall windows into a sophisticated nook, where sleek upholstered banquettes border a handsome country-style table.

ABOVE In the large dining area, the addition of L-shaped banquette seating makes the room perfect for relaxing and dining.

BELOW In a sunny nook within easy reach of the kitchen island, a rectangular-shaped space accommodates a table with a banquette and chairs.

chapter 2

eat-in styles

A freestanding island, the modern take on yesteryear's kitchen table, can be as multifunctional as the space it occupies. Serving as the visual centerpiece of this craftsman-style eat-in kitchen, a stone-topped island does double duty as the cook's prep surface and a gathering spot for family and friends.

Gathering around the dinner table is a longstanding family tradition as satisfying as the meal itself. Short on space? These days, a lack of square footage shouldn't prevent anyone from pulling up a chair. Savvy designs and modern appliances can give even the smallest kitchen the right eat-in credentials. And while a table for ten won't do in a galley kitchen, a table for two is a perfect fit.

A great **eat-in kitchen** begins with a **layout** that maximizes the **efficiency** and **beauty** of your space, factors that are significant when meal preparation, **cooking, dining,** and **cleanup** are done in **full view** of each other. The **work triangle** is a major doctrine of **good** kitchen design.

The right layout maximizes the functionality and beauty of your kitchen, factors that become even more important when dining is in full view of meal prep and cooking. To smoothly integrate the many activities that will occur—often simultaneously—in your eat-in kitchen, it's important to understand one of the major doctrines of good kitchen design: the work triangle.

The triangle concept is defined by the National Kitchen and Bath Association (NKBA) as the imaginary straight line drawn from the center of the sink, to the center of the cooktop, to the center of the refrigerator, and finally back to the sink. The elements of this triad must be kept close together to minimize the cook's efforts. A tight triangle also limits foot traffic in the work space.

In a household where just one person handles most of the food preparation, the classic work triangle's total area of 26 feet—the distance between sink, cooktop, and refrigerator—provides a traffic-free zone reserved for the serious business of meal preparation. Family and friends of the cook also benefit from this type of layout because it provides ready, unblocked access to other parts of the house.

In kitchens where there are several cooks and more than one work station, the classic work triangle may need to be reconfigured. But even when the layout requires multiple triangles, your feet will be grateful if the sink and stove are steps away from one another.

Layout Options

When choosing the kitchen floor plan that works best for your needs, consider these time-honored layouts.

One-Wall Kitchen

A straightforward layout in which everything in the kitchen—cabinets, counters and appliances—lines up along one wall. A peninsula or an island can be added that can serve as a snack bar, turning the space into a more efficient L-shape.

The Corridor/Galley Kitchen

In this layout, the stove and sink face each other, so it takes just a 180-degree turn to reach either one. The galley layout is an efficient plan for utilizing limited space, but the traffic pattern cuts through its center. You may convert the galley kitchen to a U-shaped layout by closing off one end.

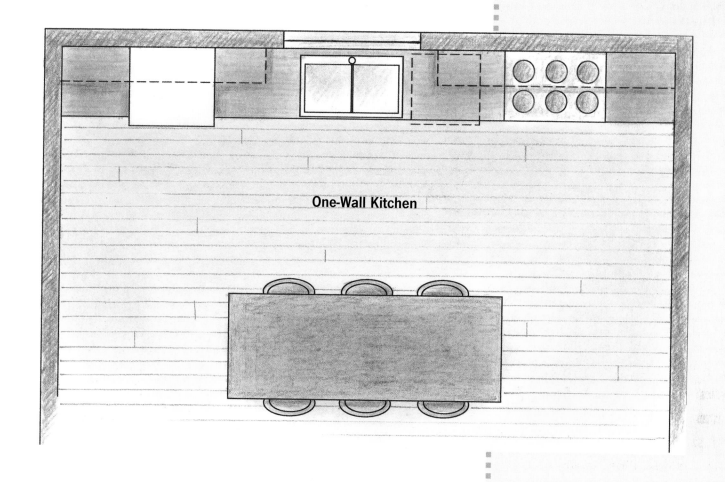

One-Wall Kitchen

TOP Often used in small apartments but also in large, open-plan homes, the **one-wall** layout requires the least amount of space. For easy access and efficiency, place the sink between the refrigerator and the range. Add an island or peninsula opposite the appliance wall for dining.

RIGHT In the compact **galley** kitchen, two parallel walls create a pass-through corridor with an efficient work triangle in the center. After appliances are in place, there should be a 48-inch-wide aisle to enable all doors to safely open. There's often room for a fold-down or café-style table for two on one wall.

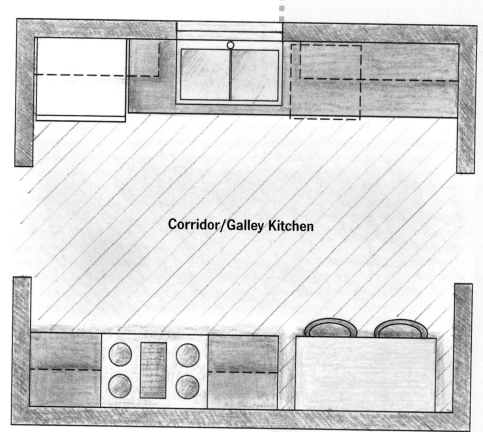

Corridor/Galley Kitchen

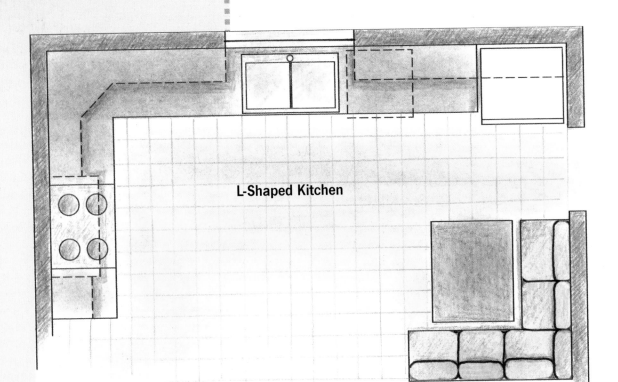

L-Shaped Kitchen

The L-Shaped Kitchen

Flexible and efficient, the L-shaped layout offers more counter space and room for dining, while it also allows easier positioning of cabinets and appliances in the classic work triangle. The best approach is to site appliances near the middle of the L, allotting enough counter space between each for prep and cooking activities. When one end of the L opens into another room, a counter and bar stools can be added. By extending cabinets along the facing wall, the L easily converts to a U-shape.

The U-Shaped Kitchen

For this layout, you'll need lots of space—at least 8 x 8 feet. The U-shaped layout is ideal for those who cook frequently because it allows for an efficient work triangle arrangement and has plenty of storage. Place a dining table at the U's opening, or open up one of its sides for a counter and stools.

The G-Shaped Kitchen

Space abounds in this layout, which is essentially a U-shape with an elongated partial leg—usually a peninsula—attached. Its abundance of countertops, storage, and floor space is a dream for multiple cooks. The U-shape also means no through-traffic and that counter space is unbroken by door openings.

OPPOSITE The **L-shaped** layout, featuring one short and one long leg, is flexible enough for two cooks to work smoothly at the same time. This layout can easily incorporate an island or peninsula for dining, as well as an ample banquette.

RIGHT The **U-shaped** layout is often praised as the most efficient, primarily because it provides a greater expanse of counter space between the sink and appliances. Another major plus is the room this layout affords at its opening for a dining table and chairs.

BELOW The **G-shaped** layout, a variation on the U-shape, incorporates a fourth leg in the form of a peninsula for meal prep and dining. There's also space here for two cooks; one work triangle may have a sink, cooktop, and refrigerator; the other may contain a second sink and oven.

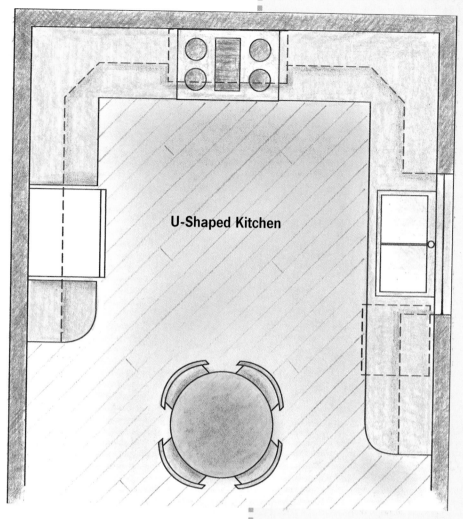

U-Shaped Kitchen

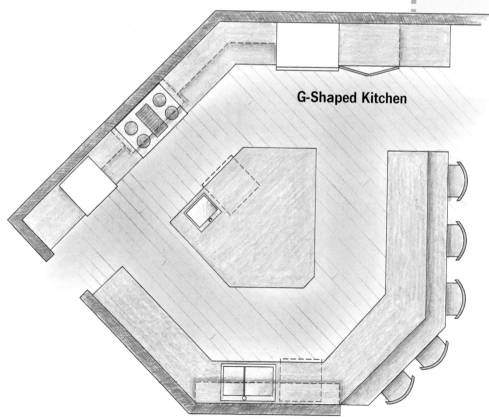

G-Shaped Kitchen

let's DISH

SPACE MATTERS

- Allow at least 18 inches and preferably 24 inches of elbow room and 12 to 19 inches of leg room for each diner at an island or peninsula.

- The bottom of the microwave should be positioned between counter and eye-level (approx. 24 to 48 inches off the floor) and be adjacent to a countertop work area.

- Include a minimum of 21 inches between counters, appliances, and cabinets for loading and unloading.

- Aisles should be wide enough for two people to pass through—at least 48 inches in food prep areas and 36 inches between facing cabinets.

Help Is At Hand

If you would like to experiment with layout possibilities for your eat-in kitchen, visit the Internet and try one of the many three-dimensional design applications available. Such programs enable you to envision an infinite number of table and seating options, countertops, cabinetry, appliances, sinks, and flooring, creating a virtual kitchen in whatever layout you fancy.

OPPOSITE TOP A two-tiered island discreetly hides the work area on one side, while accommodating diners at a lower-level breakfast bar.

OPPOSITE BOTTOM Ample space between the table and island seating areas allows guests to slide chairs in and out with ease.

RIGHT The generous expanse between the range, sink, and counters in this large kitchen allows two cooks to comfortably work without getting in each other's way.

Solutions for Small Spaces

In kitchens as in cars, size usually impacts on energy efficiency. Indeed, when a kitchen is too large, cooking a meal can become a cross-country track event. Not surprisingly, professional chefs actually prefer the compact efficiency of a galley kitchen, where the stove and sink are within easy reach on opposite walls. But while a tight layout may be optimal for the cook, it can require some design intervention to make it a viable eat-in kitchen.

Open It Up

When designed correctly, small kitchens can win the eat-in trifecta of function, beauty, and efficiency. Begin by analyzing the ways you can create more space, add storage, and welcome family and guests. One of the most popular space-adding solutions is an open-flow layout. The reason is simple: when walls and doors disappear, the kitchen flows into the dining and living areas. The benefits of such an open arrangement go beyond the enhanced social interaction between cook, family, and guests. Daily life becomes easier when the cook can simply wave a spatula to dissuade kids in the adjacent room from fingerpainting the dog.

Small spaces demand good editing. For instance, rather than lining a small space with wall-to-wall cabinets, think about adding airy, open shelving. You'll also want to pare down the number of openings into a small kitchen; too many doorways make for awkward placement of appliances and storage.

OPPOSITE Place the table near a source of natural light, if possible. Round tables are the most sociable of shapes but demand more room than other configurations.

ABOVE You can create a sense of spaciousness by adding open shelving, laying flooring diagonally, and painting the walls a light color.

ABOVE These bold, black and white floor tiles are set on the diagonal to visually expand the space.

BELOW The apron-front sink in this island has plenty of room for large platters and pots.

Solutions for increasing a kitchen's size can range from simple to elaborate. In most instances, a prioritized save-here, splurge-there approach works well. Inexpensive fixes include painting walls in light colors and adding overhead lighting to brighten and visually expand the space. You can also turn a nearby closet into a pantry for added storage, or carve a pass-through in a wall between the kitchen and the dining room. On a grander renovation scale, consider the demolition of a wall separating the kitchen from an adjacent room to allow for an island and stools for casual dining.

Making Space

There are several ways to add functional space to a small kitchen without changing its dimensions. For example, a streamlined breakfast bar along one wall fits the casual mood of a contemporary kitchen, but it can also be incorporated into a very traditional design by using the same materials for the bar and countertops.

You can gain extra work and storage space by installing deeper counters, or by building cabinets on both sides of an island for convenient storage. A sink built into an island is another smart move because it increases the kitchen's prep and cleanup space. But whether the sink is in the island or in a more traditional spot, be sure it's large enough to hold oversized pots and pans.

To enhance the feeling of spaciousness, select light-toned cabinets, countertops, and flooring. Use open shelving and glass doors. Visually expand a galley kitchen by running hardwood flooring the length of the space or by laying flooring tiles on a diagonal. And look for stoves, refrigerators, and other appliances that are designed for smaller kitchens.

ABOVE Large windows and a glass door introduce a light-filled panorama into a sunny, open kitchen.

BELOW A large island can replace the traditional table in today's eat-in kitchen.

OPPOSITE Wood stools cozy up to the island for casual seating and are easy to tuck away when not in use.

Seating Options

There are numerous seating options available for eat-in kitchens of all shapes and sizes. The possibilities include the classic table-and-chairs combination, a breakfast bar, breakfast nook, island, or peninsula. Depending on your style preference and available space, most can be adapted to fit your needs.

If the kitchen space has at least 8 feet 8 inches of clear space, you have room for a 36 x 48-inch table and four chairs. Keep family and guests seated comfortably by allotting enough room for chairs to slide in and out from under the table. For example, a rectangular table measuring 2 x 5 feet that seats six needs 2 to 3 feet of wall clearance on each side. A round table uses less space and seats more people; but be aware that if the table's radius is increased by even a small amount, the need for floor space greatly increases.

If space is tight, consider a breakfast bar, a casual and space-conserving idea for any kitchen design. For comfort's sake, the bar's overhang should be deep enough for knees to glide under; if the stools don't have footrests, add a ledge or a rail to the bar.

let's DISH

HAVE A SEAT
Comfortable seating is an absolute necessity for the eat-in kitchen. Today's simple tables and islands work with almost any chair style, so be adventurous and go for a mix of textures and materials. For example, the casual look of a bench or stool can be dressed up with fabric or leather upholstery. Add formality to wicker or wire chairs with loose seat cushions, or go modern with chrome or stainless steel.

A space-saving upholstered banquette (in essence, a bench) can be sized to slip into a kitchen nook. What's more, a banquette can work as storage when the seats are fitted with hinged lids. Use chairs on the opposite side of the table, or add another banquette to create a smooth transition to nearby space. The table can be freestanding, or it can be a peninsula that's attached to the wall or to cabinets. Giving the breakfast nook an individualized point of view is easy. Paired with a round or oval table, a curved banquette makes an elegant statement. On the flip side, you can achieve a retro look by teaming vinyl-upholstered banquettes with a laminate-topped table.

If space is too cramped for a banquette, consider attaching panels to the wall that fold down for seating. Using a drop-leaf table also makes it easy to increase dining space. You'll need approximately 220 square feet for the placement of a banquette, table, and chairs for four. Be sure, too, that your nook won't interfere with normal kitchen traffic.

Make the **most** of your kitchen space. Is there a **corner** with a sunny window? **Tuck** in a table and a **cozy** banquette.

OPPOSITE In this clever use of space, the cabinet countertop ends in a round table, making a dining spot for two.

RIGHT Tucked into a corner, the rectangular table provides ample seating with a mix of banquettes and chairs.

GREEN tip

Eco-friendly kitchen products and materials are available in an ever-growing range of styles and costs. Look for "green" countertops made of recycled tile, quartz composite—even paper or hemp.

Maximizing Storage

Taking advantage of new storage options can help small spaces hold a lot more. Begin by taking upper cabinets all the way to the ceiling to capture valuable space for items that aren't used as often as others. Put the insides of cabinet doors to work by adding hooks for oven mitts and kitchen towels. Outfit lower cabinets with helpful extras such as rollout shelves, lazy Susans, tray dividers, tilt-out bins, and chrome-plated backsplash systems with cookbook holders, spice racks, and wire baskets. To better utilize the space in deep drawers and cabinets, use pullout wicker baskets.

DID YOU KNOW?
You can have a fully coordinated kitchen right down to the insides of cabinets and drawers. It's now possible to have interior elements, such as pantry pullouts and spice racks, harmonize with the other finishes in your kitchen.

BELOW One island is fine for increased storage, but two are even better, especially when the contents are easily viewed through glass doors.

OPPOSITE Pantry-like in its proportions, this large cabinet has far less heft and a more decorative presence thanks to its glass-inset doors. Having all the dinnerware and glassware available in one convenient place is the ultimate in functional luxury.

Let There Be Light

One of life's great luxuries is the simple pleasure of sitting at the kitchen table, sipping a cup of coffee and gazing out the window. A room with a view, as it turns out, is also healthy. Researchers at Texas A&M University discovered that hospital patients who have a window in their room recover sooner than those who don't.

Whether building your kitchen from scratch or remodeling, plan to capture outdoor views and sunlight with windows or skylights. Then, plan for attractive and flexible sources of artificial light that add multiple levels of illumination to the room.

The first layer of light begins with ambient or general lighting for the whole room. Next, add lighting for tasks, and finish with decorative accent lighting. The kitchen's size and the color of its walls will help determine your kitchen's lighting needs. An all-white kitchen with high-gloss cabinets, for example, needs lower-intensity lighting than one with darker walls and matte-finished cabinetry. The number and the size of the windows will also make a difference.

Ambient or general lighting illuminates the entire kitchen and makes it possible to see into cabinets and drawers. Sources for general lighting include ceiling fixtures, cabinet uplights, recessed and track lighting, wall sconces, and table lamps. To control brightness levels, be sure to equip each source with a dimming feature.

Task lighting, on the other hand, focuses on individual work areas such as the countertop, the sink, and the stovetop, where glare-free light adds to ease of performance and safety. Pendant fixtures can also define and add intimacy to the kitchen table or breakfast nook. Banish dark spaces with under-cabinet lighting, or light the inside of glass-fronted doors.

OPPOSITE A large, granite-topped island delivers visual impact and function on many levels– from prep space to cooking area to a place for meals.

ABOVE The corner of this eat-in kitchen glows with light from the tall windows, recessed ceiling lights, and the modern chandelier.

LEFT A two-tiered island conceals the work area below the dining level.

ABOVE A colorful pair of chandeliers adds a sparkling, whimsical note to this kitchen.

OPPOSITE The clean lines of this mid-century table and chairs work well with a modern chandelier that resembles the petals of a flower.

Accent or decorative lighting adds an element of design to the room. Often brighter than ambient lighting, it is also used to emphasize architectural details, art, and displays.

Use a combination of ambient, task, and accent lighting to sculpt a kitchen that is as dramatic as it is functional. Without moving a single wall, you can make a small kitchen appear larger by using uplighting on the ceiling. If the space is narrow, open it up by bathing one wall with light. Make a kitchen with a high ceiling cozy and inviting simply by keeping light sources at lamp-shade height.

Light Fixtures

When carefully chosen to complement your eat-in kitchen's decor, fixtures serve as a source of drama, whimsy, texture, and color while they supply much-needed illumination.

Suspended Fixtures

Suspended fixtures such as chandeliers, pendants, and globes can supply ambient (general) lighting for the entire kitchen as well as for specific task areas.

Chandeliers are a classic lighting choice to hang over a dining table and can supply ambient or task lighting when connected to a dimmer switch. Chandeliers work best with ceiling heights of 8 feet or higher. The rule of thumb is that the bottom of the chandelier should hang 30 to 36 inches above the table. To avoid heads bumping into the chandelier, make sure it's at least 12 inches narrower in diameter than the table.

Pendants hang from the ceiling by a cord or pole and work extremely well over a kitchen island, lighting the workspace and looking great in the process.

Sconces may be hard to place in the kitchen because much of the wall space is used by cabinetry or furniture. So, it's best to make sure they have a purpose for being there. Use sconces as a functional source of light rather than as a solely decorative element—for example, to light up a dark area or illuminate either side of the sink.

DID YOU KNOW?
Family pets enjoy sitting near a group of people at the dining table just to be "sociable."

Surface-Mounted Fixtures

Surface-mounted fixtures attached to the ceiling or walls produce shadowless general lighting. Usually, fixtures holding several smaller bulbs generate more even lighting than those with one or two large bulbs.

A flush-mounted fixture runs level with the ceiling and adds a decorative touch without impinging on the space below. Consider it for low ceiling heights of 8 feet or less, as well as for ceilings with a bit more height.

A semiflush-mounted fixture is a good option for an 8- to 10-foot ceiling that may be too low for a chandelier but high enough that a flush-mounted fixture isn't necessary. A fine source of ambient light, the semiflush fixture makes more of a design statement than a flush-mounted one.

Recessed Fixtures

Recessed fixtures are mounted inside the ceiling or soffit. Among the variations are fixed and adjustable incandescent downlights, shielded fluorescent tubes, and totally luminous ceilings. As a rule of thumb, recessed fixtures require up to twice as much wattage as surface-mounted and suspended types.

Track Lights

Track lighting is a versatile option for general, task, and accent illumination. Modular fixtures—including artisan-crafted glass pendants—can be clipped onto the tracks and arranged to suit your needs.

OPPOSITE In this suburban kitchen, a skillful lighting plan that incorporates various types of light creates an inviting atmosphere for both dining and cooking.

ABOVE Charming pendant lights above the island, a chandelier over the banquette, and sconces flanking the sink supplement the natural light in this kitchen design.

LEFT This suspended globe illuminates the entire kitchen while providing task lighting over a table.

RIGHT Recessed downlights under the ventilation hood light the stovetop.

Tabletop Settings

The bounty of the season does as much for the tabletop as it does for the plate, telling a story that's bursting with color, shape, and texture. You can create natural centerpieces that are in step with the calendar.

Spring

A flat of cheerful pansies in wake-up shades of purple and yellow can be picked up from your local nursery. Cover the plastic flat in burlap; tie it with a slender lilac ribbon; and add moss to cover the soil.

ABOVE On an earthy farm table, bowls of fruit and a vase of hydrangeas add natural grace notes.

OPPOSITE TOP LEFT Not all fruit has to be fresh, and not all vases need be filled. This vase and over-size pear are both ceramic.

OPPOSITE TOP RIGHT Flowers don't have to sit on the table to make a dramatic impact. Tall orchids on the window ledge create the look of an indoor garden.

OPPOSITE BOTTOM Fresh pears parade down the center of the table, matching the light-hearted tone of the collectible toy display.

Summer

Pile lushly foliaged artichokes in a wooden bowl, and then randomly tuck in hydrangea blossoms or sunflowers fresh from the garden.

Fall

Parade pumpkins and gourds in all shapes and colors down the center of a long table, or line the plate of a footed cakestand with autumn leaves and stack a pyramid of miniature pumpkins on top. For a unique vase, hollow out a pumpkin, much as you would to make a jack-o'-lantern, then place a wide-mouthed glass jar inside and fill it with a flamboyant bunch of orange and yellow zinnias or chrysanthemums.

Winter

For an aromatic holiday table, weave a garland of rosemary branches down the table's center, adding a perfect pomegranate in front of each place setting. Or cover the table with a crisp white cloth and place white amaryllis blossoms and roses in a white ironstone pitcher for the centerpiece.

chapter 3

the great room

The appropriately named "great room" is the busiest spot in the house—an easy-going, convivial space where studying, snacking, TV-watching, entertaining, and just plain hanging out are conducted in full view of the cook. A well-planned layout and design makes the great room work on all levels, providing an easy flow in and out of the eat-in kitchen.

When a great room is paired with a modern eat-in kitchen, the resulting living space has the power to become the heart and soul of the home. First introduced in the late 1980s, the great room melds the kitchen, dining area, and family room into one multipurpose space. Thankfully, although shoulder pads and big hair are gone, the great room has endured, maturing into a classic.

BELOW The curved island of this dramatic eat-in kitchen gracefully leads the eye into the dining, seating, and entertainment areas of the expansive great room.

The great room concept, which often incorporates an eat-in kitchen, satisfies our desire to spend as much time as possible with family and friends. And though it may be large in some homes, the great room is not about grand scale; it's about creating an appealing place to gather and interact. From toddlers to grade-schoolers, teenagers to empty

nesters, this one space serves the evolving needs of the entire family.

Typically, planning a great room begins with its design centerpiece—the eat-in kitchen. Map out zones for cooking and food prep, storage and dish-washing, and informal dining. From there, you can carve out space for study-ing, bill paying, playing games, or putting up your feet after a long day.

BELOW The wood-framed mirror in this great room amplifies the kitchen, dining, and living areas.

BOTTOM Enlarging the doorway between the kitchen and the adjacent family room creates a great-room effect.

Design Harmony

In the best of designs, the seams don't show. In the great room, a seamless blending of zones provides uninterrupted visual unity through the entire space. Achieving a cohesive great room design can be as straightforward as repeating colors, textures, and materials throughout the space. Using similar or complementary flooring, light fixtures, cabinetry, and trim creates a cohesive, finished look. For a simple but effective renovation, kitchen cabinet doors can be removed to create open shelving that harmonizes with a similar storage display in the living area. The result is a great room that looks like a single, unified space rather than two unrelated rooms. To avoid too much uniformity and sameness, add diversity with fabrics, materials, and colors.

OPPOSITE The expansive kitchen peninsula, which can double as a cocktail bar, connects the work area with the rest of the great room.

ABOVE The view from the kitchen reveals a conversational grouping of upholstered seating flanking a fireplace, glass doors, and a striking painted screen.

RIGHT An appliance pantry created from restaurant-style shelving is hidden from the great room seating area.

Creating A Kitchen Canopy

While the floor plan may be open, the great room needs visual demarcations to keep it from looking haphazard, especially where the kitchen is concerned. Opt for design elements that differentiate the space while keeping sight lines open to and from the kitchen. Increasing the height of the kitchen ceiling with a coffered or pitched design can create a subtle visual canopy. Conversely, while a high ceiling gives the kitchen a sense of expansiveness, a low ceiling over the eating area creates an aura of intimacy.

DID YOU KNOW?

With kids and dogs running in and out of the great room, you may want to forgo vertical blinds on sliding or French doors. With heavy use, the vanes begin to fall out and bend. Better window treatment choices include roll-up blinds made of fabric, vinyl, or wood.

OPPOSITE TOP Arches create a visual boundary between the living space and this eat-in kitchen.

OPPOSITE BOTTOM A proscenium-like arch gently outlines the view of the eat-in kitchen from the living area.

RIGHT Ceiling beams accentuate the natural warmth of a country kitchen that combines burnished wood and terra-cotta tiles.

BELOW Varying ceiling heights subtly introduce two sleek, granite-topped islands into a great room illuminated with recessed fixtures, pendants, and expansive windows.

{
DID YOU KNOW?
You may position a table and chairs, a breakfast bar, an island, or a peninsula to mark where your eat-in kitchen ends and the rest of the great room begins. These are functional bridges that also work for non-eating activities
}

LEFT The island's stone countertop melds with the organic, neutral tones of the curtains, wood table, and chairs, not to mention the captivating view through the windows.

ABOVE A half-wall separates the kitchen from the living area while supplying storage and work space on the kitchen side.

RIGHT The kitchen's low ceiling rises in the living area, while a combination work island and snack bar serves as the bridge between the two spaces.

let's DISH

CONNECTIONS

The best great rooms connect the kitchen and living areas by giving them a shared design point of view.

- **At one with nature.** When removing a wall between rooms, orient the focus of the new space toward windows that bring in natural light and scenic views of the outdoors. Think of the view as framed art, compliments of Mother Nature. Place seating, such as a table and chairs or a deep-cushioned window seat, near the window, and add blinds, shutters, or curtains for sun control. Privacy needn't be sacrificed in the pursuit of light. When neighboring houses are close, windows with translucent glass serve as a screen while filling the room with lovely, diffused light.

- **Color works.** Integrate the space by carrying the color palette from the kitchen into the living area. For instance, the colors of upholstered furniture in the living space can be picked up in the tile backsplash behind the cooktop.

Cabinets as Furniture

Kitchen cabinetry and islands with the architectural detailing and quality of fine furniture are in huge demand by homeowners. Woods such as maple, cherry, ash, oak, beech, birch, or chestnut show up in a full range of light finishes for contemporary kitchens, as well as darker finishes, such as rich brown, for more formal-looking spaces. Quite often, furniture-like kitchen designs—referred to as "unfitted" pieces by English designers—feature glazed, distressed, and antique patinas that work beautifully with the rest of the great room's furniture. A hutch, for example, is a perfect piece of kitchen furniture that replaces wall cabinets as storage for dishes and glassware.

BELOW Hutch-inspired cabinetry is fitted with glass doors in a country-style kitchen; the center cabinet, designed as a baking station, has a pullout shelf for ingredients.

OPPOSITE In the space between the kitchen and living areas, a tall black cabinet serves as a bar, while the glass-paneled country cupboard holds staples.

let's DISH

FACE IT

For an elegantly cohesive look, have your cabinet-maker cover the refrigerator and dishwasher in the same material as the kitchen cabinetry. A number of appliance manufacturers design their door fronts to accept almost any custom-designed panel; others offer their own wood-overlay panels.

Integrated Appliances

The overwhelming popularity of the streamlined suite of stainless-steel range, refrigerator, and dishwasher shows no signs of lessening in its appeal. But for those who prefer to hide the kitchen's workhorses, camouflage has become an art form. While it's true that built-in appliances have been around for some time, never have they been so seamlessly integrated that it's nearly impossible to tell an appliance from a cabinet. To match the kitchen's general style, appliances are available with wood overlays and hardware. They can be so well concealed that visitors admit to needing a stethoscope to detect the purring presence of the refrigerator or dishwasher.

BELOW You can achieve a streamlined, contemporary look in the kitchen by putting the refrigerator undercover.

OPPOSITE Where's the dishwasher? It's right where it should be next to the sink, although it's cleverly disguised behind matching cabinetry.

OPPOSITE Custom wood panels match the cabinetry and disguise a side-by-side refrigerator.

LEFT In this great room, the refrigerator, hiding far left, has an overlay that's different, yet similar in style, to the nearby cabinet and fireplace.

BOTTOM Where's the fridge? It's on the far left, concealed by doors and bottom drawers that blend perfectly with the other cabinets in the kitchen.

Built-in appliances have been around for some time, but never have they been so seamlessly integrated that it's nearly impossible to tell an appliance from a cabinet.

Great Light

Enhance the view and the natural light pouring into the great room with the optimum placement of windows and French doors. A terrace connected by French doors provides not only a green focal point for the great room but also extends its boundaries. You can create a sense of continuity by constructing the great room's fireplace with the same material used for an adjacent terrace or patio area, or by extending the great room's stone floor onto the terrace. Dimmers on the great room's lighting fixtures make it possible to create just the right mood, from cozy and intimate to bright and open.

LEFT The glow from the hearth provides a warm source of light in the seating area of this great room.

BELOW Glass cabinet doors and large windows give this kitchen a bright and sunny outlook.

OPPOSITE A healthy dose of sunshine comes with the morning coffee in the comfy banquette area of this eat-in kitchen.

Flooring

No kitchen floor can do it all, but there are many options available that are great looking, durable, and easy to maintain. Appearance is a major concern when selecting flooring, but so, too, is performance. When your children are young, easy cleanup is a must. If the cook spends a lot of time standing, then comfort is key. To withstand constant foot traffic, the flooring must be durable. Ask questions, and collect plenty of samples.

Vinyl, ceramic, and linoleum are among the most affordable and durable flooring options for the kitchen. Available in sheets or tiles, resilient-vinyl flooring is presealed so it doesn't require waxing. Ceramic tiles come in a seemingly endless array of colors, patterns, and styles, and can provide a custom look with decorative borders and designs. Surprisingly, linoleum is making a comeback. This natural material composed of linseed oil and wood flour is not only eco-friendly, it has antibacterial properties.

OPPOSITE TOP The lively border pattern on this ceramic-tile floor creates a visual demarcation around the granite-topped island.

let's DISH

LOOK-ALIKE LAMINATES
If you're sold on the natural look of stone and wood for the kitchen floor but know it's not practical for your family, then laminate flooring may be your best bet. Made from paper that's impregnated with melamine, laminate looks like wood, tile, or stone but resists stains and scratches and is easy to clean. Unlike wood, laminate can't be refinished.

FAR LEFT It's time to throw out any old ideas about linoleum's humdrum, old-fashioned appearance. Not only does this updated '50s favorite add punch to an otherwise neutral kitchen, but it is an eco-friendly flooring material.

LEFT High-quality vinyl tile can replicate the look of costlier ceramic styles and has the added benefit of resilience and easy maintenance.

BELOW LEFT Less formal than marble or granite, slate tile creates a casual, textured pattern; a range of color variations give slate floors a one-of-a-kind look.

BELOW RIGHT Oversized natural stone tile is stylish and, when properly sealed, unparalleled for durability, moisture and stain resistance, and easy cleanup.

OPPOSITE Depending on how it's installed, lustrous hardwood flooring can comprise its own dynamic patterns; here, diagonal panels create a zigzag effect.

Natural stone such as granite, slate, limestone, and soapstone are unique in appearance and come in a range of earthy colors, sizes, and shapes. Durable and quick to install, laminate, a relatively new flooring product, is a spinoff from countertop materials. The look of woodgrain, stone, and other natural designs is replicated by bonding a photograph to the flooring material.

Hardwood flooring delivers warmth and a rich simplicity to any room. Though the hardwoods (oak, maple, cherry, and ash) are more durable than non-hardwoods such as pine and fir, hardwood must be refinished when its surface becomes timeworn. High-quality, prefinished hardwood flooring is becoming more popular with homeowners because it removes the annoyance of the messy floor-finishing process. Bamboo, the fastest-growing plant on earth, is a runaway trend because it's fashionable, renewable, and less expensive than hardwood.

Floor Talk

MATERIAL	EASY ON THE LEGS	WORKS FOR KIDS	PREVENTS STAINS
Resilient Vinyl	Yes	Yes	Yes
Laminate	No	Yes	Yes
Stone	No	No	No, requires special sealants
Tile	No	No	No
Wood	No	No	No, requires special coating
Linoleum	Yes	Yes	Yes

WORKS FOR RADIANT HEAT	DURABLE	MAJOR ADVANTAGE	MAJOR DISADVANTAGE
No	Yes	Easy to clean, affordable	Can lift up
Not ideal	Yes	Look of wood but easier to maintain	Can become damaged by water
Yes	Yes	Natural look and good for radiant heat	Can be slippery
Yes	Yes	Lots of looks possible	Uncomfortable for long periods of standing
Not ideal	Yes	Durable	Subject to water damage
No	No	Environmentally friendly	Narrow range of colors

OPPOSITE The granite-like texture of this vinyl sheet flooring hides footprints until you have a chance to mop.

RIGHT Laminate planks in a dark stain provide a warm, wood-like finish that stands up to the heavy traffic in this dining area.

A Place for the TV

Bigger is considered better when the subject under discussion happens to be a large-screen, flat-panel television. As this impressive form of home entertainment technology grows in popularity and drops in price, many homeowners are finding that they need to reconfigure the design of their favorite

In today's home, the broad expanse above the fireplace has become a favorite place to hang a flat-panel TV. When not in use, it's not unusual for the TV to take cover behind a painting.

viewing room. The entertainment armoires of the 80s and 90s are giving way to inspired solutions for accommodating the newest, must-have video products. Sometimes the TV takes a low-key stance and is perched behind doors of custom cabinetry positioned near the fireplace; sometimes it hangs over the fireplace with or without an art-like covering as camouflage.

chapter 4

islands and peninsulas

The island is the eat-in kitchen's anchor, drawing cook, family, and guests together to share food prep, snacks, and fellowship on its roomy platform. Below their surfaces, islands and peninsulas offer much-needed areas for storage—and ample space to pull up some comfy stools and sit for awhile.

The centerpiece of the kitchen, the freestanding island and its close relative the three-sided peninsula trace their utilitarian roots to the well-worn wooden farm table, where chickens were trussed and bread was kneaded. Designed to look good while working hard, islands and peninsulas have inherited their capacity to provide convenience, function, and beauty.

From a design standpoint, islands and peninsulas serve as geographical links to your dining and entertainment areas, while also helping to define the kitchen's borders. On a practical level, these kitchen multitaskers provide a casual place to eat or read the newspaper, as well as a staging area for food preparation, serving, cleanup, and storage. Equally important, islands and peninsulas reward the cook with the gift of open sightlines and conversational access to family and friends. They act not only as a visual centerpiece of the kitchen, but also as a social center. The island—the hands-down preference of most homeowners—can be as simple as an old pine table or as sophisticated as a custom-designed model with running water, electricity, and gas for sinks and appliances.

OPPOSITE As the center of the kitchen's action, the island often plays a style-setting role. In striking contrast to the rest of the kitchen's light-wood cabinets, this island's butcher-block top features a bold, checkerboard pattern.

BELOW A marble-top peninsula serves as a breakfast bar, while a nearby island contains a sink, prep space, and an ample area for setting out a buffet.

GREEN tip

Going green in the kitchen involves more than choosing organic foods to feed your family or eco-friendly designs and materials. To reduce landfill waste and truly connect to nature's cycles, reserve fruit and vegetable scraps for recycling into compost to feed your garden.

Island Style

While an island may be finished to match the kitchen's cabinets and countertops, many homeowners now prefer their island to look like a freestanding
piece of furniture. Harmonious—but not identical to the rest of the kitchen in
color and materials—these islands flaunt their individuality but graciously
offer extra space for dining, cooking, and storage.

If the island is to be used for casual eating—as the majority are in
today's homes—make sure the overhang measures approximately 18 inches.
Almost any piece of "real" furniture, whether new or antique, can work for
food preparation as long as it has a 36-inch-high counter. If you're designing
a custom piece to suit your exact specifications, you may—or may not—

choose to incorporate touches of your kitchen's architectural style. You'll also want to consider a finish for your island or peninsula that complements both your kitchen and the adjacent living areas.

As long as it provides the proper surfaces for eating and food prep, an island can be just about any shape. For example, depending on the size and layout of your kitchen, you might consider tossing out the traditional rectangle and going square, round, or oval. Also, think about multiple surface heights. Two-tiered islands allow you to multitask; prepare food at the waist-high work level, while at the higher counter—which conveniently keeps the mess out of sight—serve your guests. A sink can be installed on either level, as long as all code regulations are followed.

COUNTERCLOCKWISE FROM OPPOSITE
The adaptable island works on many practical levels. As a commodious, furniture-like piece, the island is a favorite spot for eat-in meals, and greatly increases the kitchen's storage potential (opposite, top). A marble-top island provides the perfect surface for the home baker (opposite, bottom); with the addition of a sink, it can serve as the prep station for a second cook (below, left); and it can be a prep and cooking site (below).

LEFT An island adjacent to a table works well, as long as there is an ample passageway between the two areas and enough space for sliding chairs in and out.

BELOW This island's generous overhang makes it easy to pull up a stool and perch comfortably.

OPPOSITE As an eat-in site, prep space, and repository for cookbooks, this island is designed for many uses.

let's DISH

ISLAND TERRAIN

- **User Zones**
  When it comes to islands, two levels are often better than one. Bar height (42 inches) is just right for eating; a lower level of 36 inches on the kitchen side hides the cooking clutter.

- **Personal Space**
  Family and guests need their space. Each person requires 12 to 15 square feet to slide a chair or stool in and out. To seat four at an island, a peninsula, or a table, you will need 48 square feet; for six, allot 72 square feet. For easy accessibility, a wall shouldn't be closer than 36 inches to seating.

- **Elbow Room**
  To avoid dueling elbows, plan on counter or table-top space of 21 to 24 inches for each diner. To keep spills from reaching undercounter storage space, add an inch to the island's overhang.

- **Roaming Radius**
  Walking space between the island and cabinets should be 36 to 42 inches. If the wall is bare, 36 inches is fine; allow for a distance of 42 inches so that large appliance doors can open freely.

Centers of Convenience

The popularity of the island has transformed eat-in kitchen design on a number of levels. For example, the old rules once proclaimed that the sink face a wall or window, which turned the user's back to those gathered around the table. Today, the sink is often part of a combination work-and-dining island, allowing cooks to simultaneously rinse dishes and chat with friends or family members perched right in front of them.

Technologically savvy islands and peninsulas, wired and plumbed for electricity, water, and gas, can add a secondary prep area to the classic work triangle. In fact, practically any appliance can be added to an island. Installed on the side facing the living area, wine chillers and icemakers make entertaining a breeze. On the kitchen side, add another dishwasher, an undercounter oven, or refrigerator drawers. And if the island is opposite the refrigerator (where most snacks originate), install a microwave.

LEFT Take advantage of the island and add another oven and sink to streamline the cooking process.

RIGHT Free up more space for bulky items in the main refrigerator by installing refrigerated drawers in the island for drinks and snacks.

{ **DID YOU KNOW?**
In a small
kitchen, an island
on wheels can be
rolled in on an
as-needed basis. **}**

Two islands can make sense in a kitchen where there is more than one cook. The primary island can be placed within the work triangle, and might contain such features as a drop-in cooktop, a microwave, refrigerator drawers, a prep sink, and a dishwasher. The second island can store china, linens, and glassware and work as a buffet table for casual entertaining.

OPPOSITE Two islands work twice as hard. Here, the center island holds the cooktop, while the second one houses a sink.

RIGHT In this twin-island kitchen, two cooks can work simultaneously because both islands feature a sink and prep space.

BELOW What looks like one large island is actually two, thanks to an end unit with storage and serving space.

ABOVE A curved island softens the flow from the kitchen to the great room, creating a sense of fluidity and casual elegance.

RIGHT The combination of stainless steel, chrome, and cool, white marble gives the island in this kitchen a sleek and contemporary look.

Layouts and Options

Because an island opens your floor plan and helps to tie all of its visual elements together, it's a key player in both traditional and contemporary eat-in kitchens. In today's designs, the island often has its own unique identity, which may be achieved by subtle differences in color and materials that complement the surrounding kitchen cabinetry.

let's DISH

PUTTING IT ON THE TABLE

If you love the utility of a two-island kitchen, but can't part with a favorite kitchen table, consider making the table a key workspace, says Ellen Cheever, CMKBD, ASID. It can be in the center of the kitchen, inviting a person to sit down while working, or be a comfortable spot to gather for a visit. Another solution is to place the table just outside the working island—long, narrow tables work very well and use space efficiently.

The island can also morph to suit your family's needs. In some homes, for instance, a large island with generous seating replaces the traditional kitchen table. Also, an island often acts as a room divider separating the kitchen from adjoining living spaces.

Go Round

Inherently social by design, a round shape allows diners to face and interact with one another. To encourage mealtime conversations, consider rounding one end of your island into a counter-height eating area. For symmetry, the opposite end of the island might also be rounded for food prep, serving, and storage. The long stretch of island in between the two rounded countertops might house a sink, a dishwasher, and a pullout wastebasket.

Two By Two

Two islands at two levels—perhaps in two contrasting shapes—add space, convenience, and visual interest to an eat-in kitchen while also facilitating a smoother flow of traffic. An oval-shaped island close to the living area might double as a place to eat and converse with the cook who is chopping vegetables at the main island. That main island might hold a sink, a steamer, and warming drawers.

Three Tiers

A triple-tiered island works well in L-shaped kitchens of any size. The first, and highest tier (42 inches), may hold a microwave and be located near the cooktop. The middle level, at a standard kitchen countertop height of 36 inches, is used as a prep and storage area. Located furthest from the work triangle, a third level (30 inches) could be rounded like a kitchen table (unlike the rectangular shape of the other two sections), and have a pedestal base—a perfect spot for serving meals and snacks.

OPPOSITE TOP LEFT Whether at the end of an island or a peninsula, a round bar table creates an excellent spot for grabbing a sandwich.

OPPOSITE TOP RIGHT A curved island can store as many appliances, utensils, and other kitchen equipment as its more linear counterparts.

OPPOSITE BOTTOM A rectangular island's marble sink surround is bordered by two butcher-block prep areas.

You can create a smooth flow around an island and maximize its workspace by designing it in a curved or rounded shape. Add a tier or two and gain lots of storage, as well as a place for a dishwasher, microwave, or wine cooler.

DID YOU KNOW?
The Mason jar was invented in New York City in 1858. The ease of its screw-top lid helped to revolutionize home food preservation, allowing families to dispense with root cellars, pickle barrels, and smoke-houses.

Focus on Furniture

When the island is crafted like a fine piece of furniture, it radiates warmth and richness. In a burnished wood such as cherry, the island pleasingly contrasts with lighter kitchen cabinetry. Whether in a traditional style filled with detailing or a sleek Shaker look, the island can accommodate stools for dining around one side of its countertop and incorporate storage underneath.

In Storage

The well-planned island greatly increases the kitchen's storage capacity simply by adding cutlery storage trays and a combination of rollout, adjustable, and open display shelves.

Curves Ahead

Curves add a sophisticated, graceful flow to a multilevel island. Areas for prep, cleanup, and casual gatherings are easily tucked into its undulating bends. Looking like an art form, yet built to function, the curved island houses such options as a built-in microwave, a dishwasher, a wine cooler, and storage.

LEFT The slight curve of the windows in this airy kitchen is echoed in the curved granite dining and prep island.

OPPOSITE This sage green island has the appearance of an antique that has been fitted with multiple storage drawers and a microwave oven.

LEFT An upholstered chair or two lend a sophisticated note to an island of any size.

BELOW The two tiers on this island, the top one of glass, the lower of granite, give the kitchen more dining space without changing its footprint.

OPPOSITE Wood chairs with woven seats add a rough-hewn contrast to the sleek granite counter.

Comfortable Seating

Eat-in kitchens are all about convenience and comfort. Maximize this comfort factor by getting the seat and table measurements just right. For example, the seat height of a typical dining chair should be approximately 17 inches; this height works with both tables and low countertops that are 28 inches in height.

An island's countertop should be 35 inches high to accommodate barstools that are 24 inches in height. Taller barstools that have a 30-inch (rather than 24-inch) seat base are an obvious choice for higher (approximately 42-inch) countertops. Keep in mind, however, that very young children can easily take a tumble from these heights. If your kitchen table has extendable leaves, make sure to allow adequate space to expand it for extra seating.

If your **kitchen table** has **extendable leaves,** make sure to allow for **adequate space** when it's time to open it up for **extra seating.**

ABOVE Hanging pendant lights make a stylish statement as they light tasks performed at the kitchen island.

OPPOSITE For maximum impact, minipendants often hang in groups above the island, creating atmosphere while serving a pragmatic function.

Lighting the Island

By surrounding the island with a mix of ambient, task, and accent lighting, the space becomes a warm, welcoming, and safe spot for kitchen tasks.

Pendant lights work as task, ambient, and decorative lighting and are especially popular for hanging over eating areas. Some pendants furnish direct downlight; others emit a general glow. As a rule of thumb, a pendant should hang about 30 inches above an island or table and be approximately 12 inches narrower on all sides. Two or more pendants make an even stronger design statement.

Minipendant lights hang in groups of two or three and add a dramatic look to a breakfast bar or kitchen island. The minilights hang from the ceiling, or may be adapted to hang from light tracks. Glass choices can be clear, opaque, and frosted in a range of shapes, patterns, and colors.

The chandelier is a fixture that hangs from the ceiling and features branched arms that hold bulbs or candles. Chandeliers and mini chandeliers, an option for smaller rooms, create a dramatic design effect.

let's DISH

LIGHT SOURCES

- A grid of recessed ceiling cans provide great general lighting

- Install individual recessed downlights as task lighting for the sink and a cooktop

- Place halogen pendant lights over bars and counters

- Under-cabinet fixtures make excellent task lighting.

Countertop Materials

Your island's countertops must not only function, but be an integral part of your eat-in kitchen's style statement. That's why you'll want to choose a countertop material as much for its surface beauty as for its durability. However, sometimes—as with much-in-demand granite—a beautiful surface requires a tad more maintenance. Fortunately, many of the countertop materials available today perform well under pressure. Mixing several types helps give the kitchen a personalized look.

Stone

Natural stone are classic beauties possessed of warmth, shimmer, and shine. Their one-of-a-kind textures, patterns, and shapes give them an aura of luxury while still being affordable.

Granite, the hardest and densest of all natural stone, is the preferred choice for kitchen counter-tops, even though its heft demands enforced cabi-net framing. It remains lustrous longer than most stone or tile, and its main mineral ingredients—sili-cates, feldspar, and quartz—fend off stains from acidic substances such as lemon, vinegar, and alcohol. Less porous than other natural stone, granite must be specially sealed every few years.

Marble is cool to the touch and offers the look of luxury for selected areas such as islands and insets in baking centers. Marble's relative softness makes it susceptible to staining, although fans of this material like the character it develops over time.

Soapstone, a frequent choice in historic homes, shows up in many modern kitchens in coun-tertops and sinks. Generally dark gray in color, soapstone stands up to heavy use. It contains talc, which gives it a smooth feel.

Slate is less porous and more durable than soapstone or marble, but does have a tendency to scratch and chip.

OPPOSITE, TOP TO BOTTOM Natural stone, such as granite, marble, and soapstone, lends a luxe point of view to the eat-in kitchen, yet performs its duties well.

ABOVE A soapstone-top island is a natural complement to the chic, monochromatic color scheme of this eat-in kitchen.

Solid-Surface Material

Solid-surface countertops are nonporous and constructed of acrylic and polyester polymers. This material is ideal for interesting architectural edge treatments or seamless countertop designs with an integral sink. Solid-surface material is stain and moisture resistant, easy to clean, and burns or scratches can be buffed out of it. There are different brands of solid-surface material available in an array of updated colors and textures.

Engineered (Composite) Stone

An extremely hard and durable man-made material, engineered stone—also called composite material—is produced by binding stone chips (predominately quartz) to powders and resins. It's fast becoming a popular choice for kitchen counters because its textured and speckled or variegated look has the visual depth of granite, and it is available in a larger range of colors. The nonporous surface, which resists scratches, stains, and heat, is easy to maintain without the annual sealing required by natural stone. Engineered stone is slightly less expensive than granite.

OPPOSITE AND BELOW Solid-surface and composite-stone countertops don't skimp on shine, yet require no annual maintenance to withstand the wear and tear of everyday use. A plus, too, is the appealing range of colors from which to choose.

DID YOU KNOW?
"The kitchen is warm and friendly, and it smells good. It's the place to live."
—Julia Child

Butcher Block

Several layers of wood are compressed together to create classic butcher block. Most commonly made of maple, oak, or birch, it is also available in exotic woods such as walnut, mahogany, and ebony. In general, wood bestows a warm look and comes in a wide range of colors and finishes. Butcher block is often used as a design detail in a single area, such as an island's countertop.

Chefs love butcher-block counters because they don't dull knife blades. However, this material's primary disadvantage is that it is porous and stains easily. In most instances, knife marks can be removed by sanding and re-oiling, but many avid cooks prefer the aged, slightly beat-up charm of a maple or oak butcher-block countertop.

Stainless Steel

Seamless stainless-steel counters—a great look for an industrial or ultramodern kitchen—can handle the punishment of moisture, heat, or a sharp knife with ease. Although stainless steel does scratch, many ardent fans appreciate the fine patina this material develops over time. It's also possible to add a finish of your choice, such as a darker tone, before installation.

Plastic Laminate

This man-made material has come a long way from its earlier days. Comprised of a plywood base covered with laminate that is applied under high pressure, it is not only the most economical countertop material, but new finishes and edges now make it more attractive than ever. A comparatively short lead time for ordering and delivery is another major plus. Certain laminate designs mimic granite, solid-surface materials, engineered stone, ceramic tile, and hardwood. Although it can stain, scorch, chip, and scratch, and water may cause warping and lifting of the substrate, the good news is that laminates are affordable to replace.

Concrete

The biggest countertop trend in recent years, concrete—a hardened mixture of water, cement, sand, stone, and pigment—is a prized look for clean-lined industrial and contemporary designs as well as gently aged farmhouse looks. While it's available in several colors and finishes, the most preferred is its natural gray state. Concrete countertops are pricey due to complicated and time-consuming fabrication, and they can crack. However, recently developed products are more durable while retaining concrete's unstained look and feel.

CLOCKWISE FROM OPPOSITE BOTTOM Countertop materials in their many varieties include the shimmer of stainless steel opposite, bottom); the warmth of wood or wood lookalikes (opposite, top); and concrete in both rough (left) and smooth finishes (above).

GREEN tip

Kitchen countertops made of recycled materials are all the rage. Consumers can choose from repurposed glass, aluminum, fiber, and even paper. These eco-friendly choices are functional and often stunningly beautiful.

chapter 5

cooking with color

Splashes of color can add personality, zest, and liveliness to any surface in the kitchen. Who can resist grinning happily at the sight of an orange range?

In eat-in kitchens everywhere, nature's palette provides an ever-changing still life: a bunch of purple grapes spilling out of a bowl; hand-fuls of green herbs awaiting their turn in a sauce; a sun-set-hued mango ripening on the windowsill. Color can also be a delicious ingredient on the walls, floors, islands, and appliances in your kitchen. In fact, many of the latest kitchen designs brim with bold, confident color.

Today, many homeowners have determined that color in the kitchen has been on the quiet side for far too long. What's their response to that age-old question about future resale value? It's often a blithe "we'll choose what we like now, and repaint later."

Color experts declare that no color is off-limits in the kitchen. The reason is that any color can be warmed up, cooled down, darkened, or lightened to suit your particular space. Even purple is showing up in kitchens in a range of soft to almost bright variations. Other strong colors such as cobalt blue, pink, turquoise, orange, red, and popular lime green are also making the culinary scene.

However, integrating color into your eat-in kitchen doesn't mean you need to focus exclusively on eye-popping hues. Warm but less-intense tones such as apricot, gold, and terra-cotta are terrific in kitchens because they stimulate the appetite while making everyone feel comfortable. And more subtle colors create a soothing atmosphere that blends well with relaxed meals. Finally, earthy neutrals, such as wood and stone, always look fresh and sophisticated.

Color by Degree

The adjectives for color run up and down the temperature scale, from hot to cold and warm to cool. Rather than measuring physical heat, these descriptive terms allude to the psychological effect color has on the observer. For instance, warm colors stimulate feelings of excitement and energy; cool colors encourage calm and relaxation. Neutral colors—the great unifiers—pull the visual environment together, eliminating distracting elements.

OPPOSITE Warm up the kitchen with a red wall and a mustard-yellow cupboard; interspersed with neutral tones, this vibrant twosome creates a sense of balanced cheerfulness.

BELOW Backsplash tiles in cool, sage green pair up well with the warm red controls on the stove.

Warm Colors

The reds, yellows, and oranges of the color wheel warm up the body's senses. Adrenaline is revved, blood pressure rises, and the breathing rate increases. "Sunset" colors stimulate appetites and give your kitchen a warm, welcoming feel. However, vibrant red, yellow, and orange can chill out when blue joins in the mix. Even cool colors heat up when combined with colors in the warm palette.

Cool Colors

Blue, green, and purple are designated as cool colors. Look at them and your heartbeat slows, muscles relax, and your body's temperature drops. They are calming and soothing and—as a result—encourage a reflective mood. Yet the degree of coolness in this color range can be tempered, depending on what type of color you blend with it. More blue in the mix and the color appears cooler; more red, and it's warmer.

Neutral Colors

Matchmaking neutrals such as brown, gray, white, and black get along well with most colors. Pale, earthy browns such as taupe and khaki elicit feelings of security, while grays act as a calming companion. Currently, a soft, almost misty, gray is being touted as "the new neutral." Go-with-everything white can be warmed up or chilled down by the addition or red, yellow, or blue.

OPPOSITE This kitchen draws its natural warmth from the brilliant floral backsplash and the butter-yellow cabinetry.

RIGHT Warm tones picked up from the wood floor and brick fireplace complement the cool green on the kitchen walls and door frames in the great room.

BELOW A bit of red wall peeks out from behind the green pottery collection, making the small space above this window pop with color.

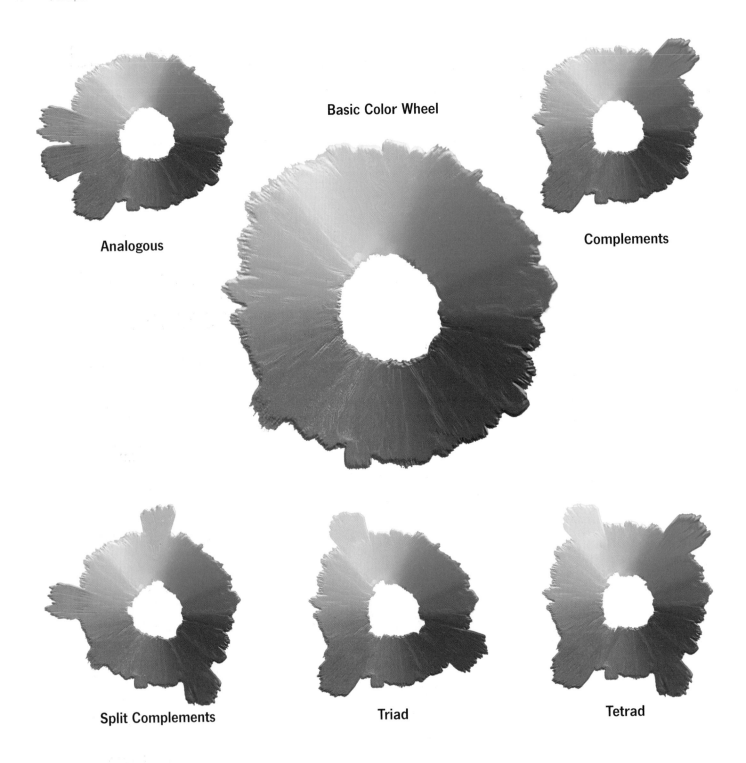

Basic Color Wheel

Analogous

Complements

Split Complements

Triad

Tetrad

Eye on Color

Learning color's descriptive vocabulary enables us to communicate what we have in mind. And, while mixing color is as much an art as a science, the right words can help you streamline your search. An additional aid to the color selection process is the exotic-looking, but simple-to-use color wheel, which was designed with color harmony in mind.

Speaking of Color

Hue and color are interchangeable words. Full-strength, undiluted color is known as a **pure** or **saturated** hue. When a pure hue is mixed with white, the result is called a **tint**. Conversely, mixing a pure hue with black or any other dark color creates a **shade**. A tint or shade of a color is known as a **tone**. **Value** alludes to the relative lightness or darkness of a color. **Intensity** refers to the saturation, strength, or brightness of a color.

On the color wheel, the three **primary** colors—red, yellow, and blue—are blended to create **secondary** colors of green, orange, and purple. Mix a primary and secondary color and the result is six **tertiary** colors.

When thinking in terms of a color scheme, there are words to help you say what you mean. **Monochromatic** defines a scheme that's comprised of one color in a range of shades and tints. Soothing and harmonic, the monochromatic color scheme is an enduring classic.

If a scheme is created using three colors that sit next to one another on the color wheel, the scheme is **analogous**. These colors always work well together because they are related and, as a result, are more harmonious.

Complements appear opposite one another on the color wheel—red and green, purple and yellow, for example—and each intensifies the other. These combinations result in a high-contrast, high-energy color scheme.

A variation is the **split complementary** color scheme, which uses a range of analogous hues that are "split" from a basic key color, with a complementary color serving as contrast. One example of a split complementary is green paired with red-purple and red-orange.

A **triadic** color scheme results when any three colors are equally spaced around the color wheel. Such a trio makes a bold, vibrant color scheme. In short, with each step up from monochromatic to analogous to complementary to triadic color schemes, a bit more energy and interest is added.

Often used because of its varied possibilities, a **tetradic** color scheme uses four colors and arranges them into two complementary pairs. In general, the four-color scheme works best when one color is dominant and attention is paid to creating a balance between warm and cool hues.

Balance plays a major role in successful color schemes. Too much of one intense color may be wearing over time, but that problem can be avoided by using a complementary color scheme. Because complementary colors are opposite each other on the color wheel, what results is a ready-made, harmonious pairing of a warm hue with a cool hue.

Two main colors are more than enough to create a satisfying kitchen color scheme. Pick your leading duo, and then add **subtle interest with neutrals;** or create **variations—lighter, darker, warmer,** or **cooler—** of your **two central colors.**

First Steps

Ready to choose a color scheme but don't know where to begin? Start by thinking about your favorite color, the one that pleases you most. Let your eyes wander for inspiration. Is there a pillow with color combinations you love? A painting, favorite scarf, vase, sweater, or dish? You get the picture. Use that object as your jumping-off point. You may need to combine a bright color—such as lime or orange—with less-intense harmonizing colors, but in the end you'll have the scheme you want.

Think about the colors of existing cabinets, countertops, and flooring. If these items are neutral—and most are because of concern about resale value—their quiet tones may give you the artistic license to add some

BELOW The vibrant mix of warm and neutral colors in the mosaic-tile backsplash complements the colors of the stone countertop.

OPPOSITE The style and colors of this stained-glass cabinet—used to store kitchen spices—is inspired by the soft green of the surrounding walls.

excitement. Consider drawing from the rich color of an upholstered chair in a nearby room. Don't be inhibited; paint is inexpensive and can be changed easily. What's more, most kitchens don't have much wall area that can be painted. So don't worry that strong colors will be overpowering; use the color that makes you feel like dancing.

Take color cues from cabinets and countertops. Examine the stain color on your cabinets to see if it has a yellow or a blue base. To prevent the walls from clashing with the cabinets, be sure to select paint colors that have the same base. If the cabinets are a lustrous cherry and the countertops are colorfully patterned, select a hue in the countertop, or choose a rich shade that works with the wood, such as French blue or light terra-cotta. For cabinets in a lighter wood, a classic scheme of olive green and deep red could add visual punch.

Draw upon the colors of the natural surroundings in the region where you live. It's a design technique that always works. For example, the Pacific Northwest leans toward warmed tones of blue and green; while the sunny Southwest likes citrus tones of orange and lime. And coastal dwellers in warm climates are drawn to tropical colors as well as aquatic blues, yellows, and greens.

Go for mood-inducing color. Cooler shades of red such as raspberry, fuchsia, and deep pink can add energy and drama to a room. To create an

OPPOSITE The drama of red and black ratchets up the kitchen's sophistication level. Here, glossy ceramic tile and matte walls add zing to black cabinets and warm wood tones.

RIGHT Neutral colors snap to attention when partnered with a bit of bold color; the blue of the hanging pendants works magic for this kitchen.

BELOW Dramatic striations in the granite countertops and backsplash connect harmoniously with the cabinets, wood trim, and stainless steel in this kitchen.

BELOW Classic black and white goes from formal to sunny when paired with yellow walls.

OPPOSITE Cool green works beautifully as a neutral, especially when it's accompanied by warm tones like those in the bamboo shade and the oak knife holder.

upbeat, social mood, orange shades put a smile on walls. Green manages to make space look both cheerful and calm. And subtle shades of blue make rooms appear more formal, which works well with traditional decors.

Add a twist to classic white. How do you make white look more current? Combine it with color, especially color in the form of bold patterns and geometric shapes.

Put it in neutral. Color experts tell us that the presence of neutral colors conveys a sense of stability. Some popular neutral shades, such as brown and dark gray, reflect the popularity of environmental materials, such as concrete, wood, and bamboo in the home. Indeed, a heightened eco-consciousness has made green the newest neutral color, particularly in mid-range tones of fern, palm, pine, and sage. The green neutrals work well alone or may be combined with blue or aqua, sandy tan, or adobe brown. Other neutrals include soothing silver and stone gray.

Pick a
Favorite Color

While still more art than science,
the psychology of color is beginning
to get serious attention. The ancient
Chinese and Egyptians believed that
color had the power to heal. In
today's world, the practice of chro-
motherapy is a type of alternative
medicine that draws upon color and
light to balance energy in the body,
whether physical, emotional, or spir-
itual. Color consultants, who practice color psychology, maintain that
specific colors evoke certain physio-
logical, as well as psychological,
reactions from most people.

    For example, while warm colors
such as red are seen as active and
exciting, blues and greens are
considered soothing and passive.
Physiologically speaking, reds are
assumed to raise body tension and
stimulate the autonomic nervous
system. Cool colors, on the other
hand, are believed to release tension and evoke feelings of calm and
relaxation.

    But in the end, the guiding prin-
ciple for selecting the "right" color
is how you feel about it. If green
energizes you while red makes you
feel sluggish, then green it is. As
you'll discover on the following
pages, every color has the power
to enchant and delight.

"The pendulum has swung back from the bland beiges of the 90s to more color and romance. A can of paint can change the whole outlook of a room."
—Mario Buatta, interior designer

Calm and tranquil, this kitchen gets its serenity from earth- and sand-colored neutrals that are juxtaposed against the cream cabinetry.

Yellow:

Good morning sunshine, welcoming, exuberant, delightful, mellow

Yellow is sunny by nature, whether it shines in bright lemon, honey gold, mustard, banana, or vanilla. Decide if you like your yellow warm—rich and saturated—or if you prefer it cool—mixed with a bit of gray or plenty of white. Balance yellow's natural exuberance with warm earth tones and cool neutrals—and, of course, with white.

Orange:

Confident, friendly, spirited, appetizing, zestful

Orange adds zest to the kitchen, so why not team it with equally flavorful accents of papaya

yellow, lime green, or spicy brown? Lighten orange with white and it becomes peach; darken it with a bit of black and it's an earthy, clay color.

Red:

Pump up the volume, the appetite, the pleasure, the vitality

Light a fire in the kitchen by adding hot spots of spicy red. Warm the entire area with a single red wall; slide red chairs under the table; top the range with a red hood; or go for major impact and have the refrigerator spray-painted red at an auto shop.

OPPOSITE TOP The sun always shines in this yellow kitchen, where the warm tones of maple cabinets and granite countertops add to the mellow image.

OPPOSITE BOTTOM The red tile backsplash enlivens the neutral tones of stainless steel and stone.

ABOVE The warmth of the cabinetry pairs well with the glossy surfaces of the sink and granite countertop.

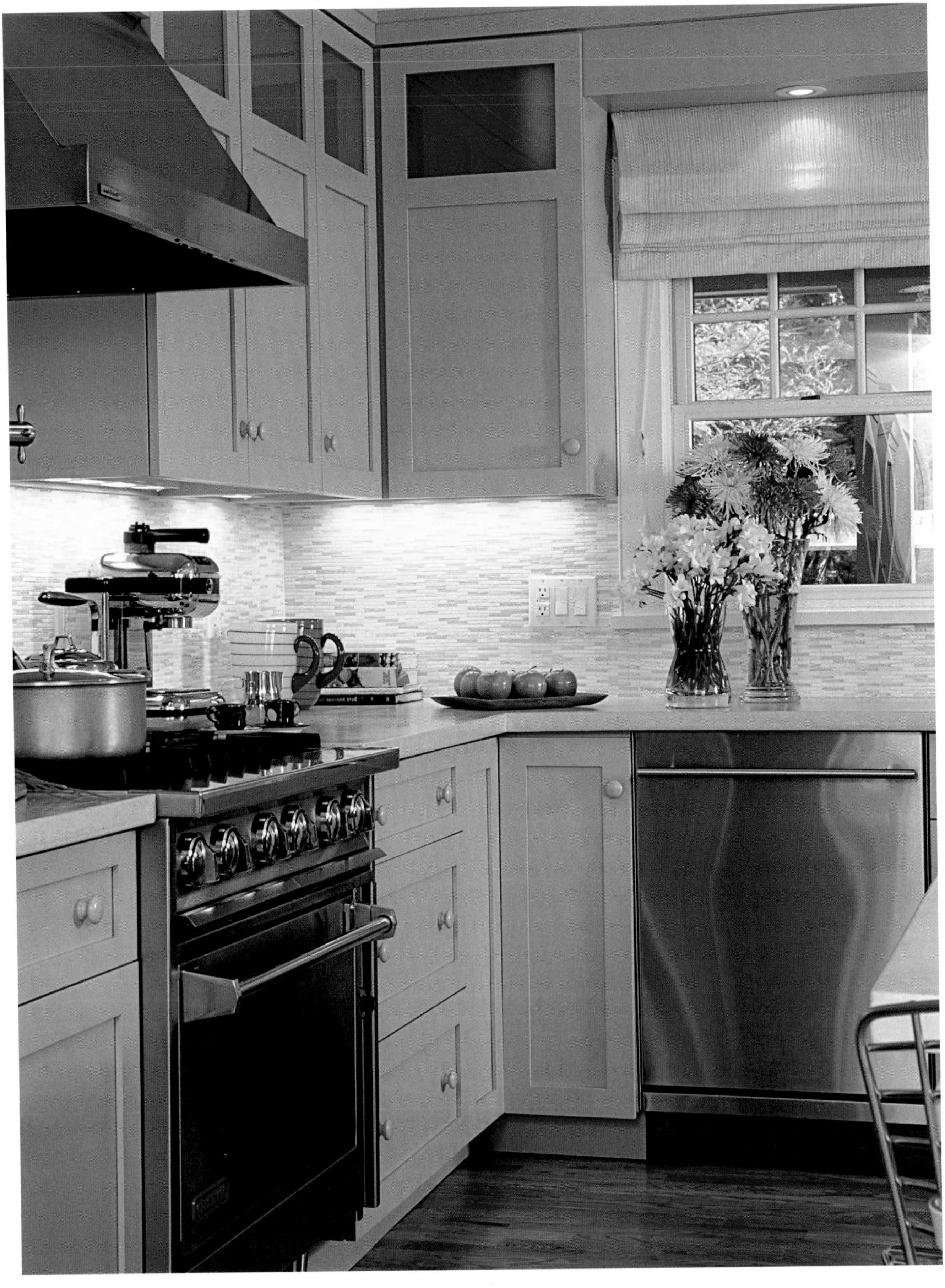

Purple:

Pour on the charm, the magic, the intensity

Think eggplant, plum, periwinkle, or iris. Purple hues create a sense of drama in the kitchen, making it the perfect backdrop for entertaining and being entertained. Taupe, tobacco brown, and crisp white make great supporting players.

Blue:

Water, clear skies, freedom, new beginnings

Keep the kitchen light and airy in mid-tone ranges of blue. Not pale, not bright, but just-right blues that suggest turquoise seas and azure skies. Make the blues sing with yellows in the same mid-tone range and you'll never want to leave the kitchen.

Green:

Nature, renewal, hope, rest, balance, sanctuary

Slow down the world. Go green. This "new neutral" can be as lively as lime, as sophisticated as sage, or as soft and calming as moss. Trim any green with white and the resulting look is one that refreshes and rejuvenates.

OPPOSITE The tranquility of seafoam green permeates the atmosphere of this kitchen, where traditional cabinets cozy up to sleek stainless-steel appliances.

ABOVE RIGHT Green in a range of tones complements pops of red and yellow in this warm kitchen.

RIGHT The high-contrast black and white in this kitchen gets an added dose of drama from the vivid, periwinkle walls.

BOTTOM Shades of gray and brown on the wall and tile backsplash get a lift from white cabinetry and an island topped in wine-colored stone.

BOTTOM RIGHT The dark-brown hutch and island are the source of visual contrast in this white kitchen.

OPPOSITE TOP The combination of black and white—the most classic of pairings—gives this kitchen a formal white-tie-and-tails insouciance.

> **DID YOU KNOW?**
> A guiding principle for selecting the right colors for your eat-in kitchen is how good they make you feel.

Brown:
Warm, calm, organic, classic, modern

Rich, yet down to earth, brown gets along beautifully with other colors, often serving as the connecting link in a design palette. On its own, brown has a color repertoire that embraces some of nature's most bewitching neutrals. Choose from a wide range of tasteful and pleasing tones, such as stone, clay, cinnamon, oatmeal, taupe, and espresso.

Gray:
Sophisticated, confident, subtle, versatile, timeless

Layer tints and shades of gray to make the kitchen glow. Add touches of crisp white and grassy green for a look that is naturally luxurious and spontaneous. Versatile gray covers the entire color spectrum, from warm yellow to cool purple tones. Whether in a traditional or modern setting, gray works.

Black and White:

Elegance, simplicity, drama, mystery, purity

High-contrast black and white is the design equivalent of the classic top hat and tails. All breezy sophistication, the duo can serve as the well-bred backdrop to the kitchen's furnishings or take center stage in grand style. Go classic with clean white walls and black countertops. Or make black and white look casual by adding a warm khaki to the walls, clean white on the moldings, and touches of black here and there.

On the Surface

Walls are only one part of the total color picture. Equally responsive to color are floors, countertops, and backsplashes.

No doubt the largest canvas in the kitchen is the **floor**, where bold-colored tiles or laminates can make a dynamic statement. Even a neutral-toned floor can be assertive with the placement of a few colorful tiles here and there, or a border that serves as a decorative accent.

The **center island** is a prime spot for dramatic color, especially when surrounding countertops are in neutral tones.

Backsplashes are another means of creative self expression. Sometimes they serve as a canvas for vibrant splashes of color in the kitchen. They might also showcase a custom-made mosaic that draws from other colors in the room. Sometimes, backsplashes are organic in appearance, featuring tumbled marble or limestone in muted, neutral colors. White subway tiles currently reign as the favored backsplash material. They are popular in small kitchens because they visually expand the space.

Refrigerators and ranges offer new metal finishes such as bronze and titanium, colorful alternatives to stainless steel. Black is in demand because it blends well with wood; while white is a perennial that never seems dated. Today's look-at-me colors, however, turn appliances into the kitchen's focal point. From subtle khaki to retro turquoise, refrigerators and ranges turn up in a color wheel's worth of shades and tints. On its own, a cobalt-blue commercial range adds a measure of personal flair to the kitchen. Of course, you can have your color now and change it later with removable color panels designed to slide into the fronts of the dishwasher and refrigerator.

OPPOSITE As the focal point of most kitchens, the island is a good place to add contrast. In this all-white eat-in kitchen, the island's gray granite countertop and stainless-steel stools and hardware add a cool touch of neutral color.

BELOW Add a fun-loving note to the kitchen by choosing an appliance, like the red stove here, in a wake-up-and-sing primary color.

let's DISH

PRIDE OF PLACE

Every eat-in kitchen has its unique brand of charm, courtesy of its owners and the items that are important to them. Whether it's an ironstone dough bowl or a hanging lineup of stainless-steel utensils, they add a personal note. Simply set your collections and treasures on high shelves and low surfaces so that whether you're sitting or standing the eye can feast on them.

Colorful Details

Faucets, once dominated by chromes and neutrals, now sport new finishes that add a dash of color to the kitchen. Copper, for example, lends a warm presence to the sink area in traditional kitchens. In modern kitchens, faucets appear in brushed stainless steel and in colors that enhance the space's design scheme. To avoid tarnishing, discoloring, or fading, the new faucet finishes are strengthened with titanium.

Add colorful hardware handles to cabinets for an inexpensive, easy-to-change update. Functional and decorative, small appliances such as mixers, blenders, and toasters look extraordinary in a wide range of hues, from soft to bold.

Kitchen accessories—tablecloths, napkins, canisters, glassware, dishes and candles—all are wonderful for finessing a color scheme.

BELOW A farmhouse sink in natural copper glows amidst black cabinetry.

OPPOSITE Color is used sparingly but makes a big impact in this white kitchen, where contrast is derived from the black farmhouse sink and the graphic rug.

chapter 6

beat the clutter

While cabinetry helps define an eat-in kitchen's style, its primary function is storage. Quite simply, cabinets are the kitchen's organizational backbone; where the vast majority of culinary paraphernalia finds its place, either behind doors, inside drawers, or on shelves. Take time to learn about the art of cabinetry and the many options available for keeping clutter out of sight.

Hide-and-seek wasn't meant to be played in the kitchen. Who hasn't stumbled on the saucepan, but not its lid? Peered into dark corners for a cake pan? Thrashed about in a drawer for the corkscrew? If your kitchen storage system isn't up to snuff, clutter and its friend, frustration, are hard to beat. Fortunately, cleverly designed cabinets, shelves, and drawers will help you win the game.

Whapter's hen dining, prepping, cooking, and cleaning up are all conducted in one space, the need for serene and systematic storage becomes more important. But before you refurbish existing cabinets or purchase new ones, be sure to examine your current scheme. Decide what organizational accessories should be added or changed. This chapter's mission is to help you in the pursuit of great-looking, service-oriented cabinetry that cuts the clutter in your eat-in kitchen.

Design Focus

As clothes make the man, cabinets make the kitchen. Cabinetry sets the tone and broadcasts your distinct style.

In essence, kitchen cabinets are storage units, yet because so many are needed, their exteriors serve as the unifying design focus of the eat-in kitchen—and often the adjoining living spaces. When it comes to finishes, many of today's homeowners are requesting furniture-like styling. But rather than going for a formal, traditional look, many opt for casual designs that reflect their approach to life. Wood cabinets—often in maple, cherry, or oak—are top choices. Popular alternatives to wood include affordable, easy-to-clean laminates in a variety of colors and patterns. Stainless-steel cabinets are not just a glistening presence in contemporary kitchens; they work well in traditional spaces with wood trim or glass inserts.

OPPOSITE Floor-to-ceiling maple cabinetry with stainless-steel hardware delivers a warm, yet modern, feeling to this eat-in kitchen.

BELOW Cabinets in pale wood tones partner beautifully with rich granite countertops and a glass mosaic-tile backsplash.

GREEN tip

Eco-friendly bamboo is great for cutting boards, backsplashes, and flooring.

let's DISH

ABOUT HARDWOODS

- **Maple** is a light-colored, medium-to-hard wood with a fine texture and even grain. Known for its shock resistance, it is highly durable and takes any stain well. It can be finished to resemble more expensive hardwoods, such as walnut and cherry.

- **Cherry,** also called fruitwood, is a strong, fine-grained hardwood with a pink undertone that is considered by many to be a luxury wood. To highlight its mahogany-red tones, cherry often has a medium or dark finish. Cherry's innately rich coloring darkens with age and exposure to light. It resists warping and is easy to carve and polish. Fine-grained hardwoods, such as maple and alder, often substitute for cherry.

- **Oak** is a heavy and open-grained hardwood found in both red and white varieties. Of the two, red oak (also known as black oak), which has a pinkish cast, is used more frequently. White oak has a slightly greenish cast. Highly visible rings and large pores give oak a coarse texture and pronounced grain. Oak stains well.

Alternatives to traditional hardwoods:

- **Alder,** part of the birch family, is a softer hardwood. Its consistent color, stability, and uniform acceptance of stains and finishes make it a preferred wood for kitchen cabinetry. Alder's natural elasticity is ideal for carving furniture-like details. It offers the look of many fine hardwoods yet is more affordable.

- **Beech** is a heavy, pale-colored, medium-to-hard wood with a fine, tight grain that resembles maple or birch. Beech stains well.

Solid Appeal

One of the more surprising findings the cabinet novice will make is that the term "solid wood" generally refers to plywood covered in wood veneer. In reality, a solid-wood cherry cabinet is probably more engineered-wood than it is cherry.

Another common misconception is that sheet goods—particleboard, medium-density fiberboard, and plywood—are poor stand-ins for lumber fresh out of the forest. This is not the case; in fact, engineered woods, which are less expensive, outperform lumber in many ways. Besides absorbing moisture, lumber shrinks and swells with changes in humidity, and it may warp and crack when used in supporting roles as the sides, bottom, top, and back of your kitchen cabinets.

Many experts contend that the best cabinets are made with plywood. And here's another surprise: cabinets made of particleboard or medium-density fiberboard can surpass the quality of those constructed with plywood. Good-quality laminate cabinets, for example, can be made with high-quality, thick particleboard underneath the laminate finish. Because it can cost less than plywood, the interiors of cabinets are often made of particleboard.

Once covered with veneer or paint, all of these engineered-wood products are officially called "solid wood." And they do look just as good, yet they are substantially more durable.

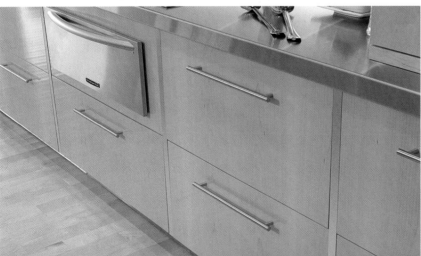

ABOVE The darker color of this wood cabinetry melds naturally with the lighter earth tones of the granite countertops, walls, and floor in this light-filled eat-in kitchen.

LEFT A striking, industrial-chic look is achieved by teaming maple cabinetry with gleaming stainless steel.

There's a **silver lining** inside **timeworn cabinets**: refinishing them isn't **very expensive**; so **redo them** in the **color** or finish you like **best.**

Fast Face-Lift

According to the National Kitchen and Bath Association (NKBA), cabinetry costs eat up roughly half of the remodeling budget. So it follows that tossing out well-built, functional cabinets doesn't make financial sense. Giving tired cabinets a face-lift does, however.

The least-expensive way to update old cabinets is to restain or paint them and add new hardware, such as hinges, knobs, and pulls. If the cabinetry's frames are good, but the doors and latches are in sad shape, the next step might be on-site professional refacing. This process, which can usually be completed in less than five days, adds a new veneer on top of the cabinet box and replaces doors and drawer fronts.

Whether painted or refaced, refurbished cabinets mean existing counters can stay in place—a substantial savings if granite or another pricey countertop material was added only a few years ago. However, if a new kitchen layout is part of your remodeling plans, refurbishing existing cabinetry probably isn't the best solution. When an extensive remodel is on the drawing board, new cabinetry gives you much-needed design flexibility.

LEFT Adding a splash of stylish color to your old cabinets can give them a fresh, new personality

OPPOSITE Whether painting, staining, or refacing your cabinetry, remember that pale colors give a light and airy look to a space, while dark hues can make the space feel smaller and cozier.

LEFT Custom cabinetry is the haute couture of the kitchen. Made to order, it fits perfectly and can be tailored in any style and finish you fancy. Here, a furniture-like hutch has glass-fronted shelves and rows of drawers for extra storage.

BOTTOM LEFT With the addition of attractive knobs and pulls, it's hard to tell whether cabinets are custom, semicustom, or stock.

BOTTOM Many stock cabinets include "custom" features, such as glass doors, allowing you to spend your renovation budget on other items.

Manufacturing Styles

Do you want a traditional, contemporary, or period-style look for your cabinetry? Your decision will help narrow down the list of style choices, as well as provide direction to the retailer, kitchen design center, or craftsman supplying them. Cabinetry terminology, as heard in the marketplace, includes the words stock, semicustom, and custom. They describe how the cabinets are manufactured—not their quality—so examine potential purchases carefully.

Stock kitchen cabinets are premanufactured and, as a result, are limited in finishes and styles. They're available on the spot or can be quickly ordered in specific sizes, usually in 3-inch increments. While once described as "bare bones," today's stock cabinets provide luxurious options previously exclusive to custom cabinets. Stock cabinet prices, however, remain tailored for the budget conscious, leaving room for upgrades elsewhere.

Semicustom cabinets are premanufactured, but come in a wider range of options and sizes than stock cabinets, and may include interior organizers and custom finishes. Semicustom cabinets are made to order, but their standard widths may require inserts for a perfect fit.

Custom cabinets are made to order. Built to the customer's specifications, there's no limitation on size, style choices, wood grade, or finish. Consequently, they require the longest leadtime and consume the biggest portion of your eat-in kitchen design budget.

Job-site cabinets were often constructed by a carpenter or cabinetmaker at the home site in a style chosen by the homebuilder. Although cabinets are still built on site, most custom work is now done in cabinet workshops. If you would like to have cabinets built on site, ask the cabinetmaker to show you examples of their finished job-site work. The quality of the painter's finishing work also determines how good the cabinets will look.

Style Matters

Because cabinetry makes the biggest impact on your eat-in kitchen's overall look, a good starting point is to select a cabinet style that either matches or complements other architectural elements in your home. If that doesn't work for you, consider harmonizing the kitchen cabinet design with the color and decor in nearby rooms. Consider these cabinet styles:

Country cabinets range in style from casual to rustic. Wood is the preferred medium, either in its natural state or distressed, whitewashed, painted, or glazed. Color works particularly well here.

Shaker cabinets project a natural sophistication through their

simplicity and utilitarian purity. Consider flat-panel doors that are inset and flush with the cabinet frame. Knobs in the same wood as the cabinets meld seamlessly with the refined and understated design.

Arts and Crafts cabinets concentrate on natural wood tones that often have a matte finish. Wood-trimmed glass inserts in the doors can make a major contribution to this style's handcrafted aesthetic.

Contemporary cabinets, streamlined and frameless, look terrific in plastic laminates, wood veneers, enamels, lacquers, and metallic-foil surfaces. Accents of stainless steel and glass are frequent embellishments on contemporary cabinetry.

let's DISH

ON THE LOOKOUT

- Take the initial cabinet measurements yourself; when shopping around, you'll have more information for comparison.

- Look for wood grains that match from cabinet to cabinet.

- Keep an eye out for shelves that can support heavy cookware and doors that can withstand years of opening and closing

- Open drawers to see if the joints are strong and dovetailed (a classic joinery technique in which wood pins and tails interlock), rather than simply glued or stapled.

- Check that drawers pull all the way out, and feature self-closing glides.

OPPOSITE FAR LEFT Cabinets can work on many levels: the uppermost section is a great stowaway place for rarely used serving pieces; while lower cabinets function as an appliance garage, cookbook shelf, and pullout storage.

LEFT Glass panes in cabinet doors and narrow, leaded-glass inserts above the countertop lend a custom touch to a traditional eat-in kitchen.

BELOW A row of glass-fronted cabinets functions much like a pantry, storing everything from dinnerware and bowls to flour and fondue pots; the center cabinet is devoted to baking supplies and has a pullout counter for easy mixing and measuring.

OPPOSITE Glass cabinets and open shelving put contents in full view, eliminating the "it's-in-here-somewhere" opening of doors. However, such easy visibility requires sustained neatness.

Smart Storage

At its functional best, good storage makes things easy in your eat-in kitchen: easy to find, easy to reach, easy to put away, and—yes—easy on the eyes. There's an inherent beauty in a well-organized kitchen. With the right accessories, cabinets, drawers, and pantries can hold more and somehow make it look like less.

Cabinet Accessories

You don't need to be an organized person to have an organized kitchen. The right storage accessories do it for you, increasing space while adding to the kitchen's efficiency. From pasta pot to pastry brush, high-functioning racks, shelves, and dividers put everything within reach. No more hunting in deep recesses; many of today's shelves and drawers pull out all the way for maximum visibility. And these accessories not only organize space, but save it: fewer items on the countertops means more room to work.

Appliance garages. Hide small appliances (food processor, coffeemaker, mixer, toaster) within reach in an unused corner or vertical space between cabinets and countertop. A minicabinet with a tambour, or rolltop door, and a dedicated electrical outlet can conceal several appliances.

Mixer shelves. Fold-down, spring-loaded shelves swing up and out of a base cabinet for use, then fold down and back into the cabinet.

Rollout shelves. These work like drawers, allowing you to bring the entire contents forward for viewing. The perpetual search has now ended.

Racks for plates, pots, spices, and wine. In pantries, drawers, cabinets, or islands, wire and wooden racks keep cooking and serving items ready and waiting.

Base-counter drawers. This fresh way to store dishes consists of a drawer fitted with a pegboard and wooden pegs that can be spaced to accommodate different sizes of plates, bowls, pots, and pans. Some may feature a roll tray above the drawer for storing linens.

Lazy Susans and carousel shelves. Rotating shelves bring dead corner space to life. A Lazy Susan rotates in a complete circle so all it needs is a gentle spin to find what's needed. A carousel shelf serves a similar function by attaching to two right-angled doors and rotating 270 degrees for easy access. A pivoting shelf, a variation on the carousel, can be built into taller cabinets to create a pantry in a small space.

Storage can be as **visually pleasing** as it is functional. Doors can deliver a **rustic farmhouse appeal,** while loosely gathered **fabric** provides a **soft** substitute for a **door.**

OPPOSITE AND TOP RIGHT Shallow wall space has been adapted into an efficient pantry for storing glassware, spices, and cooking ingredients. When closed, the door's wrought-iron motif serves as unique wall art. Notice, too, the pantry's convenient proximity to this kitchen's prep space.

BOTTOM Pullout storage underneath a soapstone farmhouse sink is camouflaged with a crisply striped curtain.

ABOVE Where there's space, there's storage; this pullout rack provides convenient access to rolls of aluminum foil, plastic wrap, and waxed paper.

BELOW An extension arm takes the standing mixer from its storage spot to the countertop.

BOTTOM RIGHT A two-layer drawer organizes flatware by size.

FAR RIGHT At the center of this eat-in kitchen, a temperature-controlled wine cooler takes its place under the counter.

Pullout wicker and wire baskets. Add visual interest to your organization system with baskets that either pivot or pull out. Available in gleaming chrome finishes as well as warm rattan and wicker, these baskets can act as a modern root cellar, storing potatoes, onions, and apples or hold baking tools and cutlery. Some even sport convenient, removable caddy baskets.

Drawer organizers. Thoroughly compartmentalize every drawer. Dividers can organize cutlery, spices, cooking utensils, and gadgets. To further maximize drawer space, check out double-level trays.

Toe-kick drawers. Hands-free, touch-and-release latches open drawers with just a light tap of a toe.

Pullout trash and recycling bins. Under-the-sink trash receptacles slide in and out as needed; positioned under butcher blocks and cutting boards, the bins make cleanup easier. Combine trash and recycling in one easy pullout system that houses three triangular bins.

Tilt-out sink panels. Make use of the space in front of the sink to store sponges, bar soaps, scrubbing pads, and vegetable brushes. There are a range of sizes to fit sink fronts of every dimension.

Vertical dividers. Store oversize serving and cooking items, such as baking sheets, trays, and platters, while using a minimum of space.

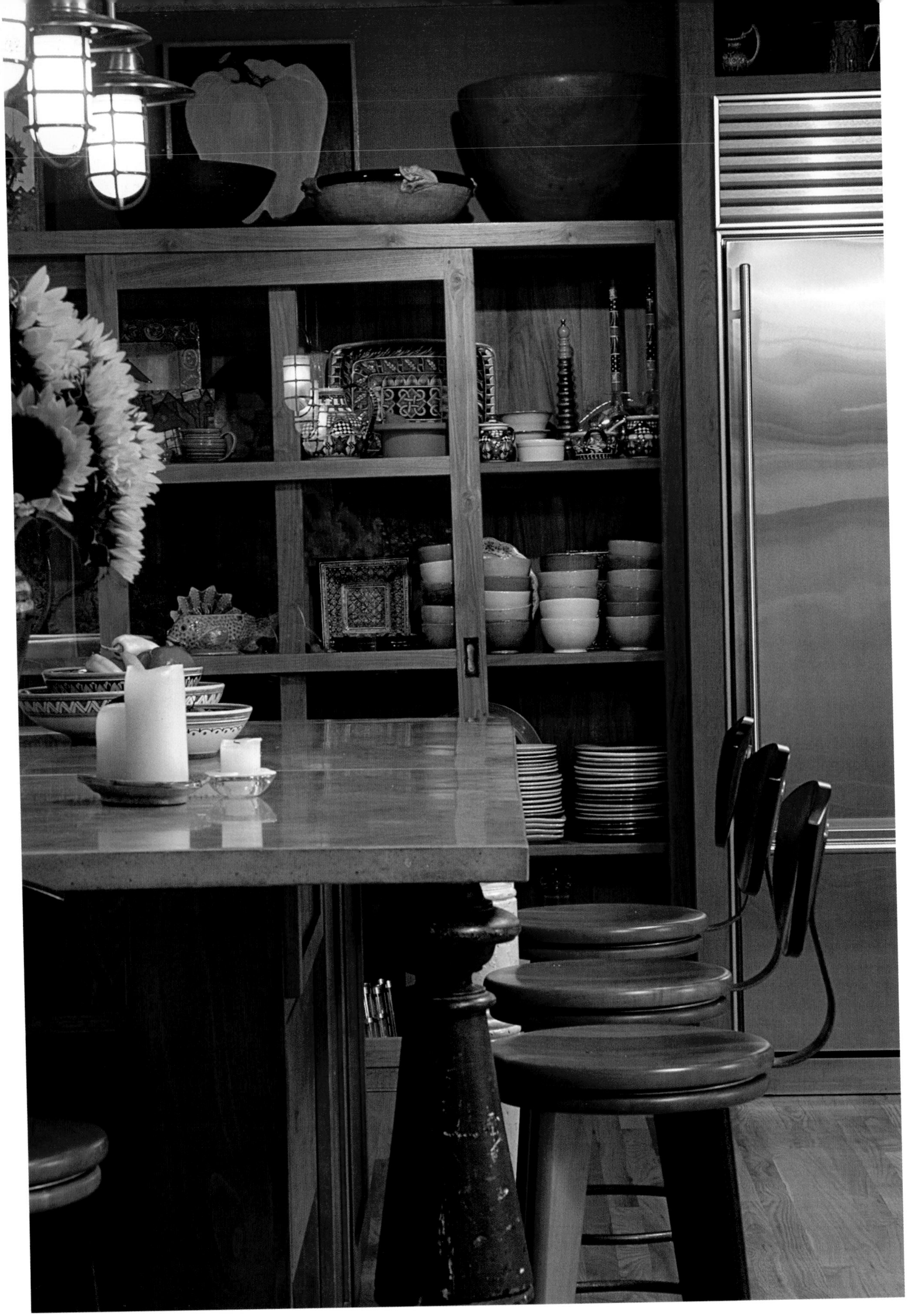

Personalized Storage

Making a unique storage statement can be as simple as adding a freestanding piece of furniture or applying a contrasting finish to a high-profile kitchen cabinet. Such an addition also provides welcome storage space to kitchens with few upper cabinets. For example, you can position an armoire near the island or dining table and stock it with serving ware, cutlery, and linens. It's a terrific way to create storage-space character to your eat-in kitchen.

Add charm to your kitchen storage with a special shelf, desk, table, china closet, sideboard, and armoire—even a bench with built-in storage. A piece of wood furniture brings a warm, cozy note into the kitchen. Look near and far for design inspiration: Asian, French Country, Shaker, or '50s Retro. What you choose may introduce pleasing architectural details, such as fluted pilasters, corbels, and moldings, or skilled handcrafted designs, such as fretwork, carved motifs, and balusters.

OPPOSITE Exuberant and extroverted, this Craftsman styled kitchen puts bright dinnerware behind the glass doors of a wood cabinet. With a weathered baluster for support and retro-style stools, the island picks up on the kitchen's light-hearted mood.

BELOW Ribbed-glass doors and under-cabinet lighting give a unique point of view to classic white cabinets.

Small in size but mighty in impact, kitchen knobs and pulls make stylish exclamation points. Great-looking hardware is often all that's needed to transform the ordinary into the extraordinary.

Knobs and Pulls

Hardware is the jewelry of cabinets, adding a personal touch of style to your eat-in kitchen. As with any jewelry purchase, decide if you want your cabinet's knobs, latches, hinges, and pulls to be understated and casual or make a grand, eye-catching statement.

Kitchen hardware is available in a vast range of classic to contemporary styles and finishes. Currently, nature-inspired motifs for knobs and pulls look particularly fresh and sophisticated when expressed in abstract design forms. A birdcage-like weave, for instance, appears in twisted stainless steel with airy open spaces; a ridged, honeycomb-like motif takes on a geometric shape in antique brass. The metals most valued for strength and durability are steel, brass, and stainless steel. Versatile steel is often plated in matte-finished copper, pewter, nickel, or antique brass or brilliantly finished as gleaming brass or polished chrome. Oil-rubbed bronze is as much in demand for kitchen hardware as it is for faucets.

In a kitchen where knobs are used on cabinet doors and pulls on the drawers, both should be selected from the same collection or—if different—be similar enough in design to complement one another. Be sure, too, that cabinetry hardware works with other metals in your eat-in kitchen design.

On the more functional side, choose cabinet knobs and drawer pulls that are comfortable to grip and easy to clean. If your hands or fingers tend to get stiff, consider C-shaped or U-shaped hardware rather than knobs.

If you'd rather forgo hardware, consider touch-and-release-style doors, or opt for doors that hang just a bit below the cabinet so they can be opened from the edge.

OPPOSITE TOP Large black pulls with the look of wrought iron lend a rustic appeal to this sleek kitchen.

RIGHT The vertical lines of these stainless-steel drawer pulls emphasize the modern design of the kitchen cabinetry.

FAR RIGHT Rustic metal takes an artistic approach in these curved, twig-like pulls on natural wood cabinets.

The Prized Pantry

The biggest resurgence in eat-in kitchen must-haves is the pantry, which is a surprising development because cabinets in new homes usually provide more than adequate storage space. Experts suggest that the pantry's appeal may be due more to its charm and nostalgia than actual necessity. In early American farmsteads, pantries (there were generally more than one) were located in the cold north corner of the house. Today, they are in—or adjacent to—the kitchen and function as a locale where bulky dry goods, appliances, and huge roasting pans can remain out of sight until needed.

The butler's pantry, minus the butler, is also back on the kitchen scene. In the late nineteenth through early twentieth centuries, when it was most prevalent in middle-class homes, the butler's pantry was also known as the serving or china pantry. Located close to the kitchen or near the wine cellar, it served as a storage and working space. In today's homes, the butler's pantry is often located in a short hallway between the kitchen and dining room. Geared for entertaining, the butler's pantry may be furnished with cabinets, a small sink, a wine cooler, and even a second dishwasher.

OPPOSITE Easily accessible, a foldout pantry makes the most of the existing space.

ABOVE Annex an adjacent space, and enjoy the luxury of a well-equipped butler's pantry.

let's DISH

ORGANIZING THE PANTRY

- **Preplan.** Set up a functional storage scheme: reserve prime real estate (eye-level to knee-level space) for items most often in demand; everything else gets nonprime space.

- **Separate all items into distinct categories, and give them their own shelf.** Canned goods have their area, as do baking products, condiments, and breakfast cereals. Those who have taken a lot of ribbing for alphabetizing their spices are on the right track. If ultra efficiency is your goal, start on the left-hand side and arrange each category of items alphabetically; for example, start the canned-goods shelf with "A" for "Appetizers," and end with "V" for "Vegetables."

- **As the pantry is filled, make a list of pantry accessories.** These include pullout drawers and racks that might make for better organization and increased storage.

- **Reserve less-valuable real estate (the lower shelves) for items such as paper towels and napkins, disposable plates, and cutlery.** Hefty items, such as bottled water, can go on a low shelf or on the floor. Place household cleaning products away from food and beverages.

- **Make a habit of reviewing the pantry (and refrigerator) once a week before grocery shopping.** Who needs nine jars of anchovies?

chapter 7

the healthy eat-in kitchen

Perhaps you can't buy good health, but you can certainly create an eat-in kitchen that supports a wholesome lifestyle.

Bring fresh air and sunlight into your eat-in kitchen with handsome, easy-to-open windows. Follow through on your healthful intentions with flooring, cabinetry, and countertops that have been manufactured with their impact on your family and the environment in mind.

Today's cutting-edge kitchen designs offer an innovative range of safe, eco-friendly products, such as bacteria-fighting surfaces, air-cleansing ventilation systems, and nontoxic paints, flooring, and cabinetry—all geared to your family's well being.

BELOW Opening the windows is the most direct way to add fresh air to the eat-in kitchen.

OPPOSITE TOP The wall-mounted hood conceals a ductless updraft ventilation system that draws smoke and cooking odors to the outside and pulls in fresh air.

OPPOSITE BOTTOM In a hood suspended over a cooktop, a recirculating updraft system pulls air through a grease filter and then recycles the air in the kitchen.

In addition to improving quality of life, today's health-conscious cabinets, countertops, backsplashes, floors, faucets, and ventilation systems look terrific. Once you become acquainted with the ever-expanding range of green products available for your eat-in kitchen, it's likely that you'll choose to incorporate as many as possible. Approach your new kitchen design the same way you would prepare a nourishing meal for your family: select the healthiest ingredients you can find, and combine them in a way that is enticing and visually appealing. And because a sun-filled kitchen is the warmest welcome, be sure to plan for an abundance of natural light streaming through windows and skylights. As you'll see on the following pages, healthy design works on all sorts of levels. Salud!

Ventilation

Only the cat enjoys waking up to the smell of last night's flounder. Fortunately, good kitchen ventilation banishes odors and grease and replaces stale air with fresh.

Mounted over the cooktop, a range hood of sufficient size and power pulls in moisture, smells, and smoke and exhausts them through a duct to the outside. Even when the weather outside is frightful and opening a window isn't an option, the ventilation system still does its job of providing fresh outdoor air. In the process, the system also controls mold-producing steam and moisture generated by cooking and dishwashing, dilutes chemical emissions and gases from building materials in the home, and reduces pet dander and dust. Some of the more expensive ventilation systems also act as safety-conscious watchdogs, activating automatically when heat is sensed. Another helpful feature offered by a number of systems alerts the owner when the filter needs a good cleaning.

Range Hoods

Thanks to striking designs and state-of-the-art technology, range hoods can easily steal the eat-in kitchen spotlight. In stainless steel, copper, ceramic tile, and even wood with carved embellishments, the perfect range hood can be purchased readymade or customized to suit your particular kitchen's style, from country cottage to country estate, French Provincial to Arts and Crafts, Old World to industrial modern. The range hood is just as likely to appear over a center-island cooktop as it is wall mounted over the stove. When needed, certain downdraft systems pop up behind the cooktop to do their work, and then lower themselves out of view. Prices can vary from less than $100 for a simple wall-mounted hood to several hundred dollars for a model equipped with lights, timers, and other bells and whistles. When the hood is custom made, the ventilation system is often purchased separately.

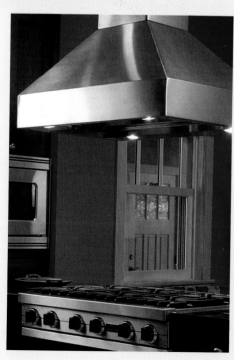

BELOW For the sake of efficiency, the stainless-steel hood extends beyond the cooktop's edge.

OPPOSITE TOP The hood, like this one clad in trimwork, often becomes the focal point of the kitchen.

OPPOSITE BOTTOM Mounted in back of the cooktop, a hoodless downdraft system draws air down and out of the house through ductwork.

Ventilation Systems

The air in well-ventilated kitchens is not only free from stale cooking odors but cleaner, which means less greasy residue on kitchen surfaces—and less cleanup. Refreshing the air in your eat-in kitchen has a design benefit as well, since many of today's range hoods are attractive works of art.

Wall- or ceiling-mounted **updraft systems** inside range hoods are the most popular form of kitchen ventilation for a good reason: the updraft system pulls smoke, grease, and moisture into the hood, ridding the house of stale air. This is achieved by exhausting the polluted air outside, or—with a **ductless** or **recirculating updraft system**—pulling the air through a grease filter (some with an optional odor-killing charcoal filter) and then recycling the cleaned air back into the kitchen. Because a ductless system does not exhaust the air to the outside, it can be an unsatisfactory choice for eliminating steam and moisture.

A third choice, the **hoodless downdraft system,** which may be installed in base cabinets close to the cooktop, uses a fan to draw air downward and vent it outside through ductwork. Downdraft systems work best over an island or peninsula cooktop where an overhead hood might not fit. Though the downdraft system is not as effective as a hooded system, it does a better job than a ductless system.

Sizing the Fan

While the hood may be gorgeous, it's the fan in the ventilation system that does the heavy work. Fans are sized according to the amount of air they can move in cubic feet per minute (CFM). The higher the CFM rating, the more air the system will move.

In general, the hood should extend beyond the edge of the cooktop and have a fan with power to properly match the hood's size. For example, a 36-inch commercial stove should have at least an 800-CFM system. When a high-powered system pulls too much air out of the house, a make-up air system, which guards against nega-

tive pressure, may be necessary. The competition for indoor air may cause appliances, such as hot water heaters and furnaces, to "backdraft," a dangerous condition that can bring harmful fumes and combustion byproducts, such as carbon monoxide into the home. As a safety precaution, consult a kitchen ventilation specialist to determine the right size for you.

Noise Control

Surprisingly, the noise from a ventilation system is not caused by the fan. The racket—which can sometimes sound like an airplane readying for takeoff—is caused by air being pulled through the filters. When shopping for a kitchen ventilation system, check the sone (sound level) rating. Ideally, you want a sone rating of 5.5 or less.

BELOW A trio of fixed windows provides an abundance of natural light and dramatic architectural elements to this eat-in kitchen.

Windows and Skylights

Sunlight streaming through the windows of an eat-in kitchen can be the most irresistible of invitations to come in, sit down, and enjoy the moment. We crave sunlight because it warms the body and feeds the psyche. And because realtors declare without hesitation that "the kitchen sells the house," it's no surprise that a home featuring a bright, light-filled kitchen

let's DISH

WINDOW STYLES

■ Fixed Windows
Designs that allow light to enter but cannot be opened.

■ Casement Windows
Often associated with midcentury and contemporary architecture, casement styles are the choice for owners of modern, retro, and art deco-style homes. Most casements open outwards at a 90-degree angle, making control of air flow easier.

■ Awning Windows
Ease of operation and the ability to solve access problems make awning windows popular. Because they open with a winding device, awning windows work well in difficult-to-reach spots where conventional double-hung windows can't be reached. In addition, an awning window can be left open without letting rain (or burglars) inside. A bonus of their outward-opening design is it doesn't interfere with living space.

■ Double-Hung Windows
An unobtrusive, popular design for most styles of homes, double-hung windows have two sliding sashes that move independently of one another. Blinds and most window coverings can be easily installed. The two sashes make it easy to control the amount of air flow.

■ Snap-in Muntins
Give single-pane windows the look of multi-pane ones with snap-in muntins. Made of either plastic or wood, the rectangular grids snap onto the back of the window or the inside depending on the window. They remove easily for window washing.

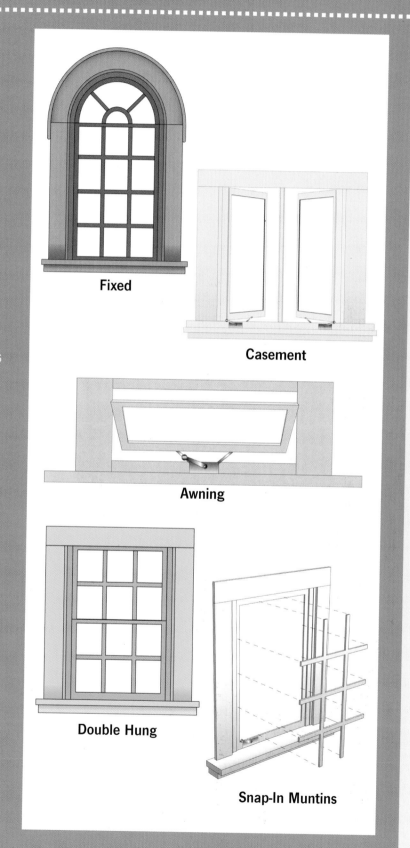

Fixed

Casement

Awning

Double Hung

Snap-In Muntins

GREEN tip

Reduce air-conditioning costs in summer by shading sunny windows with overhangs, awnings, shade screens, and trees.

ABOVE The feeling of dining al-fresco can be achieved by opening the double-hung windows that border this kitchen table.

OPPOSITE Energy-efficient windows bring light into the kitchen without wasting energy.

ranks near the top of nearly every home buyer's wish list.

The kitchen is also the room that receives the prime location in most building and design plans. No other room makes better use of natural light, capturing the sun's rays for early morning coffee, reading a recipe, finding a kitchen tool, and feeding one's body and soul until sunset.

While studies report that exposure to natural light positively affects emotional and physical health, most of us spend a majority of time working or going to school in environments with artificial lighting. No doubt that's why window installations rank so high on the list of home-remodeling projects.

Replacing or adding kitchen windows is the starting point in most kitchen renovations or redesigns. Fortunately, it's possible to bring in all the sunlight you want and do it beautifully. Although many window styles may look custom made, most are available in affordable, standard sizes.

Sometimes new windows are all that's needed to change the ambiance of the kitchen. (See "Let's Dish" page 175.) You can change a kitchen from twentieth-century traditional to twenty-first-century contemporary simply by installing sleek casement-style windows. If you want to add a sense of history to the kitchen, install double-hung windows with snap-in muntins. Stir up drama by grouping transom windows along the top of a wall. Add a bay window or glass doors near the table area. Make a sunlit statement using a large bank of windows to create a wall of glass.

There's a window style for every sensibility, too. The gardener can install a greenhouse window and keep plants—and thumb—green year-round; the architecturally inspired homeowner might choose to feature a Frank Lloyd Wright-style leaded-glass window.

When selecting windows for the kitchen, keep your home's design in mind. Choose new windows that match or are compatible with the existing ones. Because windows are grouped in a pattern, be sure the exterior look of the house is not adversely affected by adding new ones.

Examine the view from the window. The neighbor's driveway isn't high

on anyone's list of favorite sights. However, a view of nature—no matter what season—is always pleasing. Improve a good view with a larger window. Add light and make a style statement with the addition of an arched design. Window treatments can help define a room's style as much as they control natural light.

Select energy-efficient windows that require minimal maintenance. A wood-frame window with a vinyl-coated exterior supplies good energy efficiency, low maintenance, and the appeal of a natural-wood interior finish.

"Open the window, please" is a simple request, and one of the most cost-efficient methods for keeping the air fresh in your eat-in kitchen.

DID YOU KNOW?
Limit the size and number of east- and west-facing windows to keep down heating and cooling costs. Shades on south-facing windows can be added in summer, then removed to welcome the sun's heat in winter.

Skylights and Roof Windows

Operable skylights and roof windows can be excellent alternatives to more traditional windows. Not only do they look wonderful, but they also preserve your kitchen's wall space. Experts also claim that skylights can supply up to 30 percent more light than vertical windows, and if that's not enough of a selling point, they make the kitchen appear larger.

Windows installed along a roof slope or on a flat roof are generally unreachable. However, venting (operable) skylights that are hinged at the top can be operated with an electric wall switch, motorized or manual handcrank, or remote-control device to control fresh air and ventilation. Roof windows (the term is sometimes used for operable skylight as well) are generally set lower in the roofline than skylights and, as a result, are easier to reach. Their sashes are designed to pivot so that the outside glass can be cleaned from inside the house. Overall, the views from windows and skylights bring nature closer and improve moods. A ceiling fan can quietly circulate the air they provide throughout the kitchen.

DID YOU KNOW?
Lighten the heft of your energy bills by as much as $400 annually by replacing single-pane windows with Energy Star-qualified windows. These windows use low-e (low-emissivity) glass, which helps reduce year-round heating and cooling costs.

OPPOSITE Room-brightening roof windows add light without using up valuable wall space.

BELOW Skylights work as part of an overall lighting scheme that incorporates chandeliers, windows, and recessed downlights.

BELOW Because of its nonporous surface, a stainless-steel counter-top ensures that bacteria doesn't stand a chance.

Sanitary Surfaces

Nonporosity is crucial for keeping food preparation and cooking surfaces sanitary. Porous materials absorb water and increase the chance of cross-contamination from growing bacteria. Healthy, nonporous, and eco-friendly choices for countertops and backsplashes are abundant, including stained concrete, glass, fired clay, stainless steel, copper, vitreous china, and certain

imported and indigenous stone, such as granite, provided it is sealed. All are water-resistant, durable, and rely on nontoxic natural pigments. Nonporous soapstone, an indigenous stone, is also resistant to acids and alkalis; its natural patina can be maintained organically by applying mineral oil.

Countertops made from recycled paper or glass are not only sanitary green materials but are often uniquely attractive. Whatever your choice, make sure the material is well sealed to prevent staining and that countertop seams are a minimum of 2 feet away from the sink.

Antimicrobial Countertops and Backsplashes

Composite stone—usually quartz bonded with powders and resins—is a popular engineered option to indigenous stone. It is completely nonporous and never requires sealing. In addition, manufacturers of composite-stone countertops now offer antimicrobial protection that prevents the growth of harmful bacteria and molds. Keep in mind that while this feature guards against the most common bacteria, yeasts, molds, and fungi that cause stains and odors, it is not designed to protect users from disease-causing microorganisms such as salmonella.

Bacteria-Fighting Tiles and Grout

Some natural stone tiles now have antimicrobial protection and a permanent waterproofing treatment mixed in during the manufacturing process. This process makes the tiles resistant to stain-causing mold and mildew.

Copper, a Natural Antimicrobial

Copper, a soft metal, is long-wearing yet can dent and scratch fairly easily. It's determined by the eye of the beholder whether such tendencies give it character or lessen its appeal as a countertop material. A major plus is that copper is resistant to minor staining. However, copper's greatest advantage is that it's a naturally antimicrobial material. Experts tell us that untreated copper has

BELOW Composite-stone countertops, which are totally nonporous and never need sealing, contain antimicrobial protection against bacteria and molds.

BOTTOM Granite is a healthy and eco-friendly choice for countertops and backsplashes.

powerful natural antimicrobial properties, as does stainless steel (another hygienic countertop material). Using salvaged copper is a good way to save money and also help the environment. Many older homes have copper kitchen countertops, so look for demolition work in older neighborhoods.

Hands Off

Who hasn't tried to turn on the faucet without cross contaminating it with messy hands? Thankfully, there's no longer a need to wrestle with the faucet handle. Hands-free faucets, ubiquitous in public places, are now appearing in home kitchens. Not only are they more sanitary, but hands-free faucets are also an eco-friendly windfall, automatically shutting off the water when the sensor detects it's not needed. Other hands-free developments include trashcans, soap dispensers, and light switches. Could hands-free cooktops and refrigerators be next?

Breathing Easy

Volatile organic compounds (VOCs) produce potentially harmful gasses that not only reduce air quality but may be detrimental to health. The best defense is to abstain from buying building materials, finishes, and cabinetry that emit formaldehyde and other noxious chemicals. Opt instead for zero- or low-VOC products. Though cabinets made with particleboard or fiberboard may contain urea formaldehyde; they can be sealed with low-VOC paints, stains, or finishes. If your plan calls for new cabinets, check out solid-wood cabinet lines that have low-VOC emissions. As another option, choose cabinetry made with wheatboard or strawboard, combinations of agricultural fibers and sustainable binders that work best in areas that don't get wet. A majority of major cabinet manufacturers now offer eco-friendly cabinetry lines with zero VOC off-gassing.

Keep in mind that wall paints and finishes may contain high levels of VOCs. Opt for the many low- and no-VOC paints available wherever most paints are sold. Most are nearly odor free.

On the Floor

Because vinyl flooring can emit chemical fumes, safer choices are stone, tile, natural linoleum, or reclaimed wood. While cork and bamboo are the reigning alternatives to endangered wood species, such as mahogany and teak, reclaimed wood has an innate beauty of its own. Aged timbers are supplied from old mills and barns, river bottoms, swamps, even pickle vats. Visit the Internet to find reclaimed wood, such as quarter-sawn antique heart pine, sinker cypress, antique white oak, pickle-vat redwood, barn red oak, barn white oak, American chestnut, and tobacco-barn beech.

BELOW
Reclaimed wood is a superb way to create floors that are aged to perfection.

Remodel and Recycle

There are salvage yards in nearly every locale. Their main mission is to recycle used building materials. Simply do an Internet search for those recycling organizations closest to you and find out how to dismantle and donate your old cabinetry, countertops, and other reusable materials. Habitat for Humanity, for instance, operates retail centers throughout the United States and Canada called ReStores, which sell used and surplus building materials donated by building supply stores, contractors, and other supporters to the public at a fraction of normal prices. Proceeds from those sales help build decent, affordable housing for families in need.

GREEN tip

The U.S. Department of Energy puts the kitchen in perspective: its lighting, refrigeration, and cooking are ravenous users of energy, gobbling up 41.5 percent of a home's total consumption. What's more, this figure doesn't include the energy used to make hot water or to heat and cool the kitchen. All the more reason to plan for efficient home energy use. Some Energy Star-qualified appliances incorporate advanced technologies that use 10 to 50 percent less energy and water than standard models.

chapter 8

eating in style

H as the eat-in kitchen become the modern living room? Unlike the parlors of old, which were often little-used, formal

A little bit country and very much contemporary describes this sunny eat-in kitchen, where white walls and beams pair up with sleek granite countertops. A cupboard with glass doors and shelving is centered between a wall of windows, making it appear as if the trees are growing behind the glassware.

spaces that were cordoned off from daily traffic, today's eat-in, cook-in, entertain-in kitchen is a bright, busy, bustling hub where the family's real life takes place. The eat-in kitchen has a lot of living to do, and today's homeowner wants to set the stage in great style.

No other room in the home serves so many needs for so long. Because you'll spend so much time in your eat-in kitchen, you'll want to choose a style you can live with for a while. So fire up your design point of view and get cooking!

Traditional

Elegant and often a bit formal, the traditional kitchen relies on classic architecture for its grace notes. The traditional kitchen can celebrate period styles from around the world, covering designs that range from American Federal to Arts and Crafts, Neoclassical to English Victorian. Sophisticated details and materials abound: crown moldings, raised-wood paneling, gleaming dark woods, and brass hardware. To keep the design aesthetic in the forefront, it's not unusual for the traditional kitchen to mask the fact that it's really a well-equipped workspace, often hiding appliances behind handsome cabinetry. Typically, countertops are highly polished stone, such as granite or marble; flooring is usually stone or wood. Oversized cabinets, commodious islands, and jewel-like chandeliers add to the air of rich abundance. The traditional kitchen has an aura of uncluttered elegance, generally limiting itself to well-integrated displays of china or silver. And in the manner of a more formal living space, the traditional eat-in kitchen may be accessorized with Oriental rugs and artwork.

OPPOSITE AND BELOW The more formal traditional kitchen often hides appliances, such as refrigerators, dishwashers, and wine coolers, behind handsome cabinetry. Here, chandeliers hang above granite countertops, and an Oriental rug and striking artwork seem right at home.

BELOW Traditional-looking wood cabinetry joins stainless-steel appliances in an open eat-in kitchen. The eating area sets the style with a glass-top trestle table and upholstered chairs in a bold pattern.

OPPOSITE Full overlay cabinets with stainless-steel pulls work beautifully with the refined simplicity of a contemporary kitchen.

Casual Elegance

Traditional eat-in kitchens can also exhibit a less-formal personality. Period details reveal themselves in natural materials and colors ranging from earth-tones to timeless white. Crown moldings, fluted pilasters, and turned legs appear on distressed or painted cabinets; rattan dining stools gather around a kitchen island; backsplashes are made of unassuming pressed tin; sinks are hammered-copper; ceilings sport wood beams. The personal touch works well here, too, including a counter-to-ceiling chalkboard for doodles and to-do lists; or a multicolor tile backsplash behind a stainless-steel cooktop.

Shaker Kitchen

The polished style of Shaker cabinetry is a favorite for traditional as well as contemporary kitchens. Superb workmanship, clean lines, and quality woods such as maple, chestnut, and butternut were the design hallmarks of the Shakers, a once-thriving religious group first established in New England, Ohio, and other parts of the country during the late 1700s. They valued order and function.

Still highly prized for its beautiful simplicity, the classic Shaker cabinet-door style consists of recessed flat panels with a thick band of wood covering the cabinet frame. Slate or wood countertops, wood knobs, and nickel or brass hardware are common in Shaker-style kitchens. The Shaker color preference for walls and textiles includes red, blue, warm yellow, and blue-green. For greater authenticity, use matte paint rather than high gloss for walls.

In contemporary kitchens, cleanlined elements such as stainless-steel appliances and simple hardware blend well with cherry, oak, or maple Shaker cabinetry, notable for its dovetailed wood joints, plain fronts, and minimal trim.

Arts and Crafts Kitchen

Craftsmen and artists formed the Arts and Crafts movement in the late 1800s as an alternative to fussy Victoriana or the rough, machine-made products of the Industrial Revolution. This style was defined by bold, uncluttered, and functional design. (Think William Morris, Gustav Stickley, and Frank Lloyd Wright.)

In today's kitchens, the Arts and Crafts style takes a natural approach through matte wood cabinetry with flat panels or glass insets. Decorative hardware might have a hammered finish. Floors can be stone tile or wide-plank oak; painted or stenciled flooring also works well. Craftsman details such as inlaid parquetry look great on countertops and islands.

ABOVE Fine craftsmanship is evident in the abundant use of wood and glass for this eat-in kitchen's handsome cabinets, windows, and doors.

let's DISH

FORMAL COUNTRY

The formal country kitchen is classic and uncomplicated. Its essential design elements are organized, well balanced, and symmetrical. White or off-white paint often gives cabinetry a uniform, straightforward presence. Regular overlay doors are frequently used for cabinets, as are beaded inserts and glass. Polished-brass or nickel hardware add a sophisticated note to cabinets.

Country

Country styles travel near and far for inspiration, from the rustic, rural North American farmhouse to France, Italy, England, and beyond. The eat-in country kitchen simply revels in sun-kissed colors, personal touches, and comfortable furnishings. Country style also maintains its welcoming sense of respite from the modern world without sacrificing high-tech conveniences.

American Country

The farmhouse eat-in kitchen is an American beauty. Its spare design is innately graceful and harmonious. Essential to the farmhouse kitchen is a big table (or island) for family and friends to gather around. Simplicity is key, so choose clean-line crown molding for the walls, and add maple or oak cabinets with a handcrafted look. A chair rail works, too. Add bead-board paneling to the island and hang a pendant light above its surface. Other country details include brick, exposed rough beams, pine-paneled walls, and aged barn boards. Butcher block and natural stone make a functional and good-looking countertop combination. Wood flooring or stone tile (or a looka-like laminate) impart a sturdy, natural feeling. For a personal touch, display antiques and collections on open shelves. Use racks to accommodate copper pots; display pottery filled with wooden spoons and spatulas in open sight on the countertop. Mix in stainless-steel appliances, metal stools, and track lights if you're so inclined.

RIGHT The American country kitchen makes good use of wood in ceiling beams, windows, and open shelving. Recycled materials work especially well here: a rustic wood baluster gives an antique finish to the peninsula.

let's DISH

AMERICAN COUNTRY

- Flat-panel cabinet doors (detailed millwork was unavailable)

- Cabinets of different yet complementary colors; worn edges

- Natural and light-toned woods, especially pine; low-sheen finishes

- Over-sized, freestanding furniture

- Open shelving

Old-World Country

Country kitchens in every part of the world are alike in their casual focus on the everyday joys of cooking and dining together. Yet each region has its own style, particularly in Europe, where the eat-in country kitchen has been centuries in the making. Beautiful in its simplicity, Old World country kitchens exuberantly reflect the beauty of the land and the culture of its inhabitants.

French Accent

Conjure up the mood of Provence with touches of poppy red, sunflower yellow, cobalt blue, meadow green, and lavender. As a pristine counterpoint, paint walls and large, ornately-carved furniture in shades of off-white, ivory, and taupe. Cabinets can be painted a glossy white or retain their natural wood appeal. Because the French country kitchen is rustic and warm, ceilings and walls can be textured stucco that's either stained or painted, paired with wood beams in natural tones. Curtains and seat cushions often use fabrics in paisley, stripe, toile, or floral prints. Floors, often of stone or brick, might be covered with wool or cotton rugs. A heavy beam might serve as the mantel for a stone fireplace. Wooden shutters are an authentic option for windows. Furniture and cabinets might have a distressed look. Consider ceramic tile for countertops and backsplashes. Group copper pots or terra-cotta pottery on shelves. Vive la France!

LEFT Open shelves filled with terra-cotta pottery add charm and warmth to the eat-in kitchen.

OPPOSITE A formal country kitchen borrows its classical looks from architecture, thanks to its straightforward, symmetrical design. The cream-colored cabinets feature glass doors.

Speaking Italian

Earthy natural tones of brown, ochre, rich gold, sunny yellow, terra-cotta, sienna, coal black, and deep blue convey the year-round warmth of the Italian hill country. A Tuscan kitchen reflects the skills developed by the ancient Etruscans in its frequent use of wrought iron and ceramics. Handcrafted and painted tiles often depict vineyards and grapes, tomatoes and olives, cypress trees and lemons. The Tuscan kitchen table, which originated in ancient Roman times, is often dark-painted oak. At other times, the table is given a single coat of white paint and scratched up a bit for an antique look. The big bonus of centuries-old Tuscan design? The sunny, comfortable look is as affordable as it is visually pleasing. This is a style that begs for repurposed over store-bought.

Tuscan families eat and cook together, so the kitchen design needs to provide plenty of room to move freely. For your Tuscan-inspired eat-in kitchen, add a wood table, and mix open cupboards with the cabinetry. Consider painting walls a rich, Tuscan red or intense yellow and trim them with molding. You might like to include a hand-painted mural as well. On the floor, choose from earthy terra-cotta tiles, glazed ceramic tiles, or marble inlays in intricate patterns. Wood floors look great in their natural color. Kitchen furniture should be substantial, strong, and functional. The kitchen sink might be white ceramic or marble. Display copper pans on racks suspended from the ceiling; use wrought iron for drawer pulls and light fixtures. Should you want to go the full distance, build a brick-fired bread oven like the ones found in large Italian farmhouse kitchens.

LEFT Spice up the kitchen with Italian-style dark wood cabinetry, colorful ceramics on open shelves, and a mosaic-tile backsplash.

OPPOSITE Victorian charm is captured here with white cabinetry, open shelves displaying floral-patterned china, and a row of open plate racks.

It's time to unpack your china and heirlooms: a wide range of display options makes it easy to include your personal mementos in the kitchen.

Kitchen English

The English country style sprang not from the estates of the landed gentry but from modest homes lived in comfortably for generations by ordinary townsfolk. The English country kitchen's contents appear to have been collected over many years, giving the room a charming, lived-in look and a connection with the past. To acquire the English kitchen's well-worn patina, avoid anything too new and shiny; cabinetry should look antique and incorporate details such as plate racks, niches, and glass fronts. On the floor, consider wood or tile in a matte finish. Countertops can be stone, solid surfacing, or wood. Colors are on the light side. Chintz fabrics are quintessentially English, as are collections of English bone china in floral patterns.

let's DISH

ENGLISH COUNTRY
- Open display racks for china
- Bead-board end panels
- Patina-creating paints and finishes
- Glass mullion doors on cabinets; doors may be flush with the cabinet frame
- Applied turned legs on islands
- Floral chintz and china

BELOW Sleek maple cabinetry and stainless steel are the driving aesthetic choices behind this dramatic contemporary kitchen.

OPPOSITE TOP A utilitarian kitchen derives its style from functional elements; small details, such as cabinet hardware, can make a big design statement.

OPPOSITE BOTTOM The Asian concepts of order and harmony merge with Western contemporary design in a kitchen that combines soapstone countertops with stainless-steel appliances.

Contemporary

Modern contemporary styles change from year to year, as evidenced by retro modern, mid-century modern, and high-tech designs. What endures is the streamlined maxim of "less is more." In the eat-in kitchen this translates to fewer accessories, hidden appliances, and minimal details. Today's modern kitchens often use stainless steel, marble, granite, and frosted glass to make a cool, functional statement. More often of late, a strong warm note is sounded with wood cabinetry in light tones of maple, cherry, and birch. Cabinetry, in general, features full-overlay doors (often referred to as European-style) that cover most of the cabinet frame; hinges are usually concealed. Basic geometric shapes and bold colors such as red, blue, and yellow—or high contrast black and white—supply visual impact.

Utilitarian Chic

Based on practicality, the designed-to-function modern kitchen is a supremely organized sweep of geometric lines. Its style announces that utilitarian is hip. Such a minimalist approach often opts for a monochromatic, clean design. Uniform cabinetry may appear in frosted glass, stainless steel, wood, or a high-gloss paint in red or cobalt blue. Hardware is either subtle or out of sight. Though few in number, details are incredibly important. Windows are bare; concrete covers countertops and occasionally the floor; lighting is suspended; and fixtures are simple in design. Open shelves hold unadorned white dinnerware. Rather than displaying personal items, carefully selected metal utensils sit ready for use.

Asian Fusion

The Asian aesthetic of balance and harmony and the West's modern design unite in Asian fusion, a style that's at once calming and dynamic. More often than not, the Asian influence is seen in the refined use of natural and renewable organic materials in a Western-style kitchen. An amalgam of woods and wood-like materials may flow in the same kitchen. An Asian-fusion kitchen may contain natural cork, which reduces the impact of standing; it appears as flooring in home and commercial kitchens. A cork floor in an open kitchen may flow into a dining area where the flooring is bamboo. Cherry wood cabinetry, in turn, harmonizes with the red hues of the variegated cork. The island is a dark wenge, while Makassar ebony shows up as a detail on a cabinet sink. The end result is a serene and tranquil—a blend of modern design with the natural and the exotic.

Asian style is a merging of influences drawn from Chinese, Japanese, Korean, Vietnamese, and Thai influences. For the most part, the West has looked to the Chinese and Japanese for design inspiration. Japanese style favors neutral, minimalist colors such as tea green and black. Chinese style, on the other hand, is brighter (lots of red) and often uses lacquer finishes. In the West, the two styles are blended into neutral settings with bold accents.

resource guide

The following list of manufacturers and associations is meant to be a general guide to additional industry and product-related sources. It is not intended as a listing of products and manufacturers represented by the photographs in this book.

MANUFACTURERS

Amana
403 W. 4th St.
Newton, IA 50208
800-843-0304
Manufactures refrigerators, dishwashers, and cooking appliances.

American Standard
P.O. Box 6820
1 Centennial Plaza
Piscataway, NJ 08855-6820
www.americanstandard-us.com
Manufactures kitchen sinks, faucets, and tile products.

Andersen Windows
100 4th Ave. North
Bayport, MN 55003-1096
800-426-4261
www.andersenwindows.com
Manufactures windows, skylights, and patio doors.

Ann Sacks Tile and Stone,
a div. of Kohler
1210 SE Grand Ave.
Portland, OR 97214
800-278-8453
www.annsacks.com
Manufactures tile and stone.

Armstrong World Industries
2500 Columbia Ave.
P.O. Box 3001
Lancaster, PA 17604
800-233-3823
www.armstrong.com
Manufactures flooring, cabinets, and ceilings.

Benjamin Moore & Co.
101 Paragon Dr.
Montvale, NJ 07645
www.benjaminmoore.com
Manufactures paint.

Bruce Hardwood Floors,
a div. of Armstrong World Industries
www.bruce.com
Manufactures hardwood flooring.

Corian, a div. of DuPont
Chestnut Run Plaza
721 Maple Run
P.O. Box 80721
Wilmington, DE 19889
800-426-7426
www.corian.com
Manufactures solid-surfacing materials.

Delta Faucet Company
55 E. 111th St.
P.O. Box 40980
Indianapolis, IN 46280
800-345-DELTA (3358)
www.deltafaucet.com
Manufactures faucets.

Elkay
2222 Camden Ct.
Oak Brook, IL 60523
630-574-8484
www.elkayusa.com
Manufactures sinks, faucets, and countertops.

Hafele
800-423-3531
www.hafele.com
Manufactures decorative cabinet hardware, architectural mouldings, and range hoods.

KitchenAid
800-334-6889
www.kitchenaid.com
Manufactures appliances, sinks, and faucets.

Kohler
444 Highland Dr.
Kohler, WI 53044
800-456-4537
www.kohlerco.com
Manufactures sinks, faucets, and plumbing products.

KraftMaid Cabinetry
P.O. Box 1055
15535 S. State Ave.
Middlefield, OH 44062
888-562-7744
www.kraftmaid.com
Manufactures stock and built-to-order cabinetry.

Viking Range Corp.
888-845-4641
www.vikingrange.com
Manufactures appliances, ventilation systems, trash compactors.

Wilsonart International
P.O. Box 6110
Temple, TX 76503-6110
Phone: 800-433-3222
www.wilsonart.com
Manufactures solid-surfacing materials, plastic laminates, and adhesives.

INFORMATION SOURCES

American Lighting Association
P. O. Box 420288
2050 Stemmons Freeway, Ste. 10046
Dallas, TX 75342-0288
214-698-9898
www.americanlightingassoc.com
The trade association of the lighting industry; includes manufacturers, retail showrooms, and lighting designers.

BuildingGreen, Inc.
802-257-7300
www.buildinggreen.com
An independent company that provides accurate, unbiased, and timely information about green design and products.

Department of Energy (DOE)
800-342-5363
www.doe.gov
Promotes national energy security through reliable, clean, and affordable energy. DOE's Web site provides free materials focused on energy consumption and efficiency.

Energy Star
www.energystar.gov
Find energy-saving products recommended by the Environmental Protection Agency and Department of Energy.

Environmental Home Center
206-682-7332
www.environmentalhomecenter.com
A catalog source for green building products.

Green Building Blocks
www.greenbuildingblocks.com
A resource for green design and product information.

National Association of Remodeling Industry (NARI)
780 Lee St., Ste. 200
Des Plaines, IL 60016
800-843-6422
www.nari.org
Professional organization for remodelers, contractors, and designers; offers consumer information.

National Kitchen and Bath Assoc. (NKBA)
687 Willow Grove St.
Hackettstown, NJ 07840
800-843-6522
www.nkba.org
Trade organization for kitchen and bath professionals that provides consumer product information and referrals.

glossary

Accent lighting: Illumination that highlights an area or object to emphasize that aspect of a room's character.

Accessible design: Design that accommodates persons with physical disabilities.

Adaptable design: Design that can be easily changed to accommodate a person with disabilities.

Ambient light: General illumination that surrounds a room. There is no visible source of the light.

Appliance garage: Countertop storage for small appliances.

Apron: The front panel of a sink that may or may not be exposed.

Awning window: A window with a single framed-glass panel. It is hinged at the top to swing out when it is open.

Backlighting: Illumination coming from a source behind or at the side of an object.

Backsplash: The finish material that covers the wall behind a countertop. The backsplash can be attached to the countertop or separate from it.

Baking center: An area near an oven(s) and a refrigerator that contains a countertop for rolling out dough and storage for supplies.

Base cabinet: A cabinet that rests on the floor under a countertop.

Base plan: A map of an existing room that shows detailed measurements and the location of fixtures, appliances, and other permanent elements.

Basin: A shallow sink.

Built-in: A cabinet, shelf, medicine chest, or other storage unit that is recessed into the wall.

Bump out: Living space created by cantilevering the floor and ceiling joists (or adding to a floor slab) and extending the exterior wall of a room.

Butcher block: A counter or tabletop material composed of strips of hardwood, often rock maple, laminated together and sealed against moisture.

Casement window: A window that consists of one framed-glass panel that is hinged on the side. It swings outward from the opening at the turn of a crank.

Centerline: The dissecting line through the center of an object, such as a sink.

CFM: An abbreviation that means cubic feet per minute. It refers to the amount of air moved by an exhaust fan.

Chair rail: A decorative wall molding installed midway between the floor and ceiling. Traditionally, chair rails

protected walls from damage from chair backs.

Cleanup center: The area of a kitchen where the sink, waste-disposal unit, trash compactor, dishwasher, and related accessories are grouped for easy access and efficient use.

Code: A locally or nationally enforced mandate regarding structural design, materials, plumbing, or electrical systems that states what you can or cannot do when you build or remodel. Codes are intended to protect standards of health, safety, and land use.

Combing: A painting technique that involves using a small device with teeth or grooves over a wet painted surface to create a grained effect.

Cooking center: The kitchen area where the cooktop, oven(s), and food preparation surfaces, appliances, and utensils are grouped.

Countertop: The work surface of a counter, island, or peninsula, usually 36 inches high. Common countertop materials include plastic laminate, ceramic tile, slate, and solid surfacing.

Cove lights: Lights that reflect upward, sometimes located on top of wall cabinets and behind crown molding.

Crown molding: A decorative molding usually installed where the wall and ceiling meet.

Dimmer switch: A switch that can vary the intensity of the light source that it controls.

Double-hung window: A window that consists of two framed-glass panels that slide open vertically, guided by a metal or wood track.

Downlighting: A lighting technique that illuminates objects or areas from above.

Duct: A tube or passage for venting indoor air to the outside.

Faux painting: Various painting techniques that mimic wood, marble, and other stone.

Fittings: The plumbing devices that transport water to the fixtures. These can include faucets, sprayers, and spouts. Also pertains to hardware and some accessories, such as soap and instant hot-water dispensers.

Fixed window: A window that cannot be opened. It is usually a decorative unit, such as a half-round or Palladian-style window.

Fixture: Any fixed part of the structural design, such as sinks.

Fluorescent lamp: An energy-efficient light source made of a tube with an interior phosphorus coating that glows when energized by electricity.

Framed cabinets: Cabinets with a full frame across the face of the cabinet box.

Frameless cabinets: European-style cabinets without a face frame.

Glass blocks: Decorative building blocks made of translucent glass used for nonload-bearing walls to allow passage of light.

Glazing (walls): A technique for applying a thinned, tinted wash of translucent color to a dry undercoat of paint.

Ground-fault circuit interrupter (GFCI): A safety circuit breaker or receptacle that compares the amount of current entering a receptacle with the amount leaving. If there is a discrepancy of 0.005 volt, the GFCI breaks the circuit in a fraction of a second. GFCIs are required by the National Electrical Code in areas that are subject to dampness.

Grout: A binder and filler applied in the joints between ceramic tile.

Halogen bulb: A bulb filled with halogen gas, a substance that causes the particles of tungsten to be redeposited onto the tungsten filament. This process extends the lamp's life and makes the light whiter and brighter.

Highlight: The lightest tone in a room.

Incandescent lamp: A bulb that contains a conductive filament through which current flows. The current reacts with an inert gas inside the bulb, which makes the filament glow.

Intensity: Strength of a color.

glossary

Island: A base cabinet and countertop unit that stands independent from walls so that there is access from all four sides.

Joist: Set in a parallel fashion, these framing members support the boards of a ceiling or a floor.

Kitchen fans: Fans that remove grease, moisture, smoke, and heat from the kitchen.

Lazy Susan: Axis-mounted shelves that revolve. Also called "carousel shelves."

Load-bearing wall: A wall that supports a structure's vertical load. Openings in any load-bearing wall must be reinforced to carry the live and dead weight of the structure's load.

Low-voltage lights: Lights that operate on 12 to 50 volts rather than the standard 120 volts used in most homes.

Muntins: Framing members of a window that divide the panes of glass.

Nonbearing wall: An interior wall that provides no structural support for any portion of the house.

Palette: A range of colors that complement one another.

Peninsula: A countertop, with or without a base cabinet, that is connected at one end to a wall or another countertop and extends outward, providing access on three sides.

Proportion: The relationship of one object to another.

Recessed light fixtures: Light fixtures that are installed into ceilings, soffits, or cabinets and are flush with the surrounding area.

Refacing: Replacing the doors and drawers on cabinets and covering the frame with a matching material.

Roof window: A window installed in the slope of a roof. Roof windows meet egress and escape requirements.

Scale: The size of a room or object.

Sconce: A decorative wall bracket, sometimes made of iron or glass, that shields a bulb.

Secondary work center: An area of the kitchen where extra activity is done, such as laundry or baking.

Semicustom cabinets: Cabinets that are available in specific sizes but with a wide variety of options.

Sight line: The natural line of sight the eye travels when looking into or around a room.

Skylight: A framed opening in the roof that admits sunlight into the house. It can be covered with either a flat glass panel or a plastic dome.

Sliding window: Similar to a double-hung window turned on its side. The glass panels slide horizontally.

Snap-in grilles: Ready-made rectangular and diamond-pattern grilles that snap into a window sash and create the look of a true divided-light window.

Soffit: A boxed-in area just below the ceiling and above the vanity.

Solid-surfacing countertop: A countertop material made of acrylic plastic and fine-ground synthetic particles, sometimes made to look like natural stone.

Space reconfiguration: A design term that is used to describe the reallocation of interior space without building an addition.

Spout: The tube or pipe from which water gushes out of a faucet.

Stock cabinets: Cabinets that are in stock or available quickly when ordered from a retail outlet.

Subfloor: The flooring applied directly to the floor joists on top of which the finished floor rests.

Surround: The enclosure and area around a tub or shower. A surround may include steps and a platform, as well as the tub itself.

Task lighting: Lighting designed to illuminate a particular task, such as chopping.

Tone: The degree of lightness or darkness of a color.

Trompe l'oeil: French for "fool the eye." A paint technique that creates a photographically real illusion of space or objects.

True divided-light window: A window composed of multiple glass panes that are divided by and held together by muntins.

Undercabinet light fixtures: Light fixtures that are installed on the undersides of cabinets for task lighting.

Universal design: Products and designs that are easy to use by people of all ages, heights, and varying physical abilities.

Wainscoting: Paneling that extends 36 to 42 inches or so upward from the floor level, over the finished wall surface. It is often finished with a horizontal strip of molding mounted at the proper height and protruding enough to prevent the top of a chair back from touching the wall surface.

Wall cabinet: A cabinet, usually 12 inches deep, that's mounted on the wall a minimum of 15 inches above a countertop.

Xenon bulb: A bulb similar to a halogen bulb, except that it is filled with xenon gas and does not emit ultraviolet (UV) rays. In addition, it is cooler and more energy efficient.

index

index

photo and designer credits

All photography by Mark Samu, unless otherwise noted:

Page 1: design: Jean Stoffer **page 4:** design: Andreas Letkovsky AIA **page 6:** design: Kitty McCoy, AIA **page 9:** design: Ken Kelly **pages 10–11:** *both* design: Big Designs **page 12:** design: Andreas Letkovsky AIA **page 13:** *left* design: Big Designs; *right* Durst Construction **pages 14–15:** design: Big Designs **page 16:** design: Carpen House **page 17:** *top* design: Big Designs; *bottom* design: Capital Construction **page 18:** design: Jean Stoffer Design **page 19:** design: Ken Kelly **page 20:** design: EJR Architect **page 21:** design: Innovative Marble **page 22:** design: Donald Billinkoff AIA **page 23:** *top* design: Blairhouse Interiors; *bottom* design: Donald Billinkoff AIA **page 24:** design: Doug Moyer AIA **page 25:** design: Susan Fredman Design **page 26:** design: EJR Architect **page 27:** *top right* design: Ken Kelly; *bottom left* design: Carpen House **page 28:** *bottom left* design: Ken Kelly; *bottom right* design: Andreas Letkovsky AIA **page 29:** design: Big Design **page 30:** top *left* design: Durst Construction; *bottom* design: Innovative Marble **page 31:** *top* design: EJR Architect; *bottom right* design: Eileen Boyd **page 32:** *top left* design: Charles Reilly Design; *bottom left* design: Andreas Letkovsky AIA; *right* design: Benvenuti & Stein **page 33:** Eric Roth **page 34:** design: Donald Billinkoff AIA **page 35:** design: Evergreen House Interiors **page 36:** design: Durst Construction **page 37:** *top* design: EJR Architect; *bottom* design: Jean Stoffer Design **page 39:** design: EJR Architect **pages 40–43:** *illustrations* Glee Barre **page 44:** *top* design: Doug Moyer AIA; *bottom* design: Correia Design **page 45:** design: Ken Kelly **page 46:** design: Doug Moyer AIA **page 47:** design: Samu Studios Inc. **page 48:** *top* design: EJR Architect; *bottom* design: Jean Stoffer Design **page 49:** design: Big Designs **page 50:** Robert Storm Architect **page 51:** design: Jean Stoffer Design **page 52:** design: EJR Architect **page 53:** design: Charles Reilly Design **page 54:** design: Donald Billinkoff AIA **page 55:** design: EJR Architect **page 58:** design: Big Designs **page 61:** *bottom left* design: Samu Studios Inc. **page 62:** design: Doug Moyer AIA **page 63:** *top left* design: Jean Stoffer Design **page 65:** Jessie Walker **page 66:** design: Ken Kelly **page 67:** *top* design: The Michaels Group; *bottom* design: Eileen Boyd **page 68:** design: Correia Design **page 69:** *both* design: Donald Billinkoff AIA **page 70:** *top* design: Charles Reilly Design; *bottom* design: Big Designs

page 71: *top* Brian Vanden Brink; *bottom* design: Ken Kelly **page 72:** design: EJR Architects **page 73:** *left* design: Artistic Design by Deidre; *right* design: Ken Kelly **page 74:** design: Jean Stoffer Design **page 75:** design: Samu Studios Inc. **page 76:** design: Donald Billinkoff AIA **page 77:** design: Samu Studios Inc. **page 78:** design: SD Atelier AIA **page 79:** *top* design: Lucianna Samu Design; *bottom* design: Ken Kelly **page 80:** *top* design: Susan Fredman Design **page 81:** Jessie Walker **pages 82–83:** *top left* courtesy of Forbo; *bottom both* courtesy of Armstrong **page 84:** *left* design: Artistic Design by Deidre; *right* Deborah Sherman **page 85:** design: Samu Studios Inc. **pages 86–87:** *both* courtesy of Armstrong **page 88:** Thomas McConnell **page 91:** design: Jean Stoffer Design **page 92:** design: Durst Construction **page 93:** design: Innovative Marble **page 94:** *top* design: Charles Reilly Design; *bottom* design: Eileen Boyd **page 95:** *left* design: Innovative Marble; *right* design: Andreas Letkovsky AIA **page 96:** *top* design: Andreas Letkovsky AIA; *bottom* design: Eileen Boyd **page 97:** design: Jean Stoffer Design **page 98:** design: EJR Architects **page 99:** design: Samu Studios Inc. **page 100:** design: Andreas Letkovsky AIA **page 101:** *top* design: Ken Kelly; *bottom* design: Jean Stoffer Design **page 102:** design: Ken Kelly **page 103:** design: Big Design **page 104:** *top left* design: EJR Architect; *top right* design: Jean Stoffer Design; *bottom* design: Innovative Marble **page 106:** design: EJR Architects **page 107:** design: SD Atelier AIA **pages 108–109:** *top left* design: Capital Construction; *bottom* design: Ken Kelly; *bottom right* design: EJR Architects **page 110:** design: Big Design **page 111:** design: Jean Stoffer Design **page 112:** *top* design: EJR Architects; *center* design: Innovative Marble; *bottom* design: Innovative Marble **page 113:** design: Andreas Letkovsky AIA **page 114:** design: Artistic Design by Deidre **page 115:** *top* design: Jean Stoffer Design; *right* design: KJB Design **page 116:** *top* design: Innovative Marble; *bottom* design: Carpen House **page 117:** *left* design: Jean Stoffer Design; *right* design: Susan Fredman Design **page 119:** design: Samu Studios Inc. **page 120:** design: Ken Kelly **page 121:** design: Jean Stoffer Design **page 122:** design: Ken Kelly **page 123:** *top* design: Donald Billinkoff AIA; *bottom* design: Susan Fredman Design **page 126:** design: Ken Kelly **page 127:** design: Jean Stoffer Design **page 128:** design: Capital Construction **page 129:** *top* design: Ken Kelly; *bottom* design: Ken Kelly **page 130:** design: Jean Stoffer

Design **page 131:** design: Eileen Boyd **page 132:** design: Artistic Design by Deidre **page 134:** *top* design: Ken Kelly; *bottom* design: Jean Stoffer Design **page 135:** design: Charles Reilly Design **page 136:** design: Robert Storm Architect **page 137:** *top* design: SD Atelier; *bottom* courtesy of Glidden **pages 138–139:** *bottom left* design: KJB Design; *bottom right* design: Samu Studios Inc.; *top right* design: Jean Stoffer Design **page 141:** design: Doug Moyer AIA **page 142:** design: Jean Stoffer Design **page 143:** design: Samu Studios Inc. **pages 145–147:** *all* design: Ken Kelly **page 149:** *top* design: Correia Design; *bottom* design: Carpen House **page 150:** design: Robert Storm Architect **page 151:** design: Eileen Boyd **page 152:** *top* design: Carpen House; *bottom left* design: Durst Construction; *bottom right* design: Innovative Marble **pages 154–155:** *left* design: Artistic Design by Deidre; *right* design: Jean Stoffer Design **pages 156–157:** *both* design: Jean Stoffer Design **pages 158–159:** *all* design: Lucianna Samu Design **page 160:** *top left* design: Doug Moyer AIA; *bottom left* design: Ken Kelly; *bottom right* design: Carpen House **page 161:** design: Jean Stoffer Design **page 162:** design: Susan Fredman Design **page 163:** design: EJR Architect **page 165:** *top & bottom right* design: Jean Stoffer Design; *bottom left* design: Carpen House **page 166:** design: Andreas Letkovsky AIA **page 167:** design: Carpen House **page 169:** design: Big Design **page 170:** design: EJR Architect **page 171:** *top* design: Big Design; *bottom* design: Capital Construction **page 172:** design: Andreas Letkovsky AIA **page 173:** *top* design: Jean Stoffer Design; *bottom* courtesy of Wolf **page 174:** design: Benvenuti & Stein **page 176:** design: SD Atelier **page 177:** design: Doug Moyer AIA **page 178:** design: EJR Architect **page 179:** design: Jean Stoffer **page 180:** design: Carpen House **page 181:** *top* courtesy of Zodiaq; *bottom* design: EJR Architects **page 183:** design: Ken Kelly **page 185:** design: Andreas Letkovsky AIA **page 186–187:** *both* design: Jean Stoffer Design **page 188:** design: Evergreen House Interiors **page 189:** design: Ken Kelly **page 190:** design: EJR Architect **page 191:** design: Ken Kelly **page 192:** design: KJB Design **page 193:** design: Carpen House **pages 194–195:** *both* design: Jean Stoffer Design **page 196:** design: Carpen House **page 197:** *top* design: Donald Billinkoff AIA; *bottom* design: Jean Stoffer Design **page 200:** design: Len Kurkowski, A.I.A. **page 203:** design: Jean Stoffer

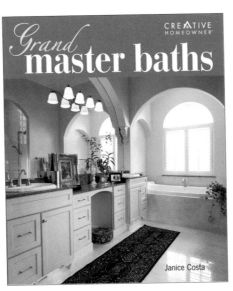

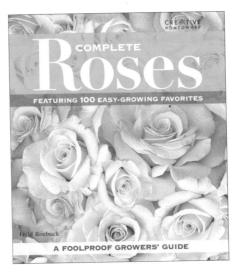
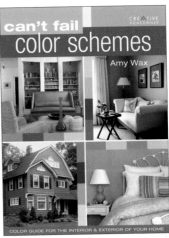